The *Horse Illustrated* Guide to

BUYING A HORSE

By Lesley Ward

BOWTIE
P R E S S

A Division of BowTie, Inc.
Irvine, California

Karla Austin, Business Operations Manager   Nick Clemente, Special Consultant

Ruth Strother, Editor-At-Large   Jen Dorsey, Associate Editor

Erin Kuechenmeister, Production Editor   Michelle Martinez, Assistant Editor

Rebekah Bryant, Editorial Assistant   Michael Vincent Capozzi, Book Design

The horses in this book are referred to as *he* or *she* in alternating chapters unless their gender is apparent from the activity discussed.

The photographs on pages 60, 64, 65, 68, 70, and 71 courtesy of © Bob Langrish

Library of Congress Cataloging-in-Publication Data

Ward, Lesley.
  The horse illustrated guide to buying a horse / by Lesley Ward.
     p. cm.
  ISBN 1-931993-16-5 (hardcover : alk. paper)
  1. Horses. 2. Horses--Buying. I. Title.

SF285.W25 2004
636.1'0029'7--dc21
                                                    2003014034

BowTie Press®
A Division of BowTie, Inc.
3 Burroughs
Irvine, California 92618
Printed and bound in Singapore
10 9 8 7 6 5 4 3 2 1

Acknowledgments

I would like to thank the following people for their help with this book: Marian Abe; Chris Avery; Pat Bailey of The Club, San Juan Capistrano, CA; Sharon Biggs; Jane Butteriss; Liz Ericson; Jane Frusher; Pat Fuchs; Paula Grimstead; Moira C. Harris; Alex and Kelly James; Denise Justice; Laura Loda; Julie Mignery; Carol Nelson; Jennifer Nice; Sherry Pasqual; Annette Slowinski, D.V.M.; and finally my father, Alan Ward, for his excellent editing skills.

Contents

Contents

American Saddlebred
Warmblood
Cross-Breed

Get on the Phone
The Visit
Questions, Questions, and More Questions

Handling the Horse
Tacking Up
Observe the Horse Being Ridden
Your Turn to Ride
The Horse's Specialty
Trail-Ride Test
Decision Time

Exam Day
The Examination Form

Where's the Horse Going to Live?
Transportation
Insurance
Handing over the Money
Welcome Home
Riding Your New Horse
Have Fun
Bill of Sale

Introduction

You may remember the first time you got on a horse's back. Didn't it feel great? You probably decided then and there to own a horse of your own one day. A few years have passed since then, but the desire to own a horse didn't go away, so why fight it?

The Horse Illustrated *Guide to Buying a Horse* helps you decide if owning a horse is really for you. You need to think carefully about whether caring for a thousand pounds of responsibility fits into your lifestyle.

If you decide to go ahead, be prepared to shop around. It takes time and effort to find a suitable animal. Beware—there are equine lemons out there, and even horses whom many consider to be good may be unsuitable for a first-time buyer. You may have to look at a lot of horses before you find one you really like.

Remember, a bad horse costs just as much as a good horse to feed and shoe. Be sure the first horse you buy is the right one for you. It's no fun having to sell an unruly or unhealthy horse a few months after you have bought him, and it's likely you'll lose money and time in the process. It's not always easy finding a suitable horse, but this book helps you make the correct choice.

Once you've found that terrific horse, you won't have to watch the clock, count precious minutes left in your riding lesson, or hand over a much-loved horse to his owner. You'll be the boss. Realizing that you're actually the proud owner of a horse is an amazing feeling, and it won't be long before you're doing the things you enjoy: improving your riding skills, jumping over fences in competition, or trail riding through the countryside.

So what are you waiting for? Start reading. This book will make your search for a horse as stress-free as possible. The perfect horse is out there somewhere, waiting for you to give him a good home.

Are You Ready to Own a Horse?

Before you start searching for a horse, think about how much of a commitment you can make. Owning a horse takes plenty of time and money. If you have a high-powered job and work eighty hours a week, do you really have the time to look after and ride a horse? If you don't have a regular income, are you able to support an often-expensive hobby?

Time

Ideally, you should be able to visit your horse at least once a day and ride him several times a week. If he's going to live at your home, you or someone you know should check on him more frequently. It takes only a few seconds for a horse to injure himself in a paddock or out in a field. And even if your horse is going to live at a boarding facility, you still need to have a close look at him at least once a day. Boarding facilities can be busy places, and although the staff may promise individual attention, no one looks after your horse quite like you do.

For health reasons, a horse needs to be groomed several times a week, have an occasional bath, and get a reasonable amount of exercise. All of this adds up to several hours a week. Do you have that time? If you keep your horse at a boarding facility, you also have to add on the time it takes to get there and the time it takes to get to work. If you already own a dog or cat, you know that keeping him or her healthy and happy takes a lot of time and effort. It's the same with a horse, perhaps even more so.

Still, if you truly want a horse, most obstacles can be overcome. If you keep your horse at home, you'll get used to getting up at 6:00 A.M. instead of 7:30 A.M. to have an hour to spend with your horse before work. Your workmates will get used to your changing out of riding clothes in the office restroom. And if you have children, they'll quickly learn that your four-legged child needs your attention too. Think about how you'll fit your new horse into your schedule before you actually start looking for a horse.

Money

Once you've decided you have the time, you must determine if you have enough money. Check your bank balance before you begin the search. How much money can you realistically afford to pay? A recreational riding horse can cost several hundred to many thousands of dollars, depending on his breeding, experience, and age. The horse's location can raise the price too. Horse prices in the wealthy areas of Southern California or the East Coast may shock you.

A horse who already excels at jumping, dressage, or reining is going to cost more than one who has stood out in a field for five years; also, the more ribbons he has won, the higher price you'll pay. A horse with top-class breeding costs a pretty penny too. Does your first horse really need a flawless pedigree? Probably not. Older horses, fourteen and over, tend to cost less than younger ones, but many have the experience a beginner needs. An older horse could give you many years of reliable riding.

At the other extreme, a young, unbroken horse may be a bargain but only for an experienced horse person who knows how to train him properly. But don't get discouraged. There are some

An experienced show horse costs more than one who has never competed.

moderately priced horses out there; it just takes a little more time to find them.

Once you decide how much you can pay, stick to your budget. Don't get overeager and let a trainer or a dealer pressure you into looking at horses who are out of your price range. Remember that trainers often get a commission from sellers, and it may be in their interest to have you pay a high price for a horse.

The purchase price is only the beginning. It's the monthly maintenance bills that you really must budget for. If you are not keeping your horse on your property, you will have to pay a monthly rent at a boarding facility. There are veterinarian and

You will need to pay a farrier every five to six weeks.

feeding bills. Do you know how much a bale of hay costs in your region? You need to have some extra money set aside in case of an emergency. If your horse gets sick or injured, the vet bills can be gigantic. You'll also have to pay a farrier to trim or shoe your horse's hooves every five to six weeks, and you'll need grooming equipment and tack: a saddle and fittings, a bridle, brushes, and other supplies. If you live in a chilly climate, you may need a horse blanket to keep your horse warm.

To get an idea about how much these supplies cost, do some investigating in your area. Go to feed stores to find out how much you are going to pay for grain and hay. Drop by a few tack shops to check the prices of saddles, bridles, brushes, and blankets. Ask friends who live locally how much they spend each month maintaining their horses. Call up a farrier or two and ask what they charge for shoeing and trimming. Chat with an equine vet to learn what he charges for annual vaccinations such as tetanus, influenza, and encephalomyelitis (sleeping sickness). Once you've gathered this important information and have written it down, you'll have a pretty good idea about how much you're going to spend keeping your new horse healthy and happy.

Do you know where your horse will live? If you're lucky, you can keep him on your property at home. If not, you will have to board him. Check out the facilities near your home. How much do they charge per month? What is included in the board? Will they blanket your horse each day in winter if you can't be there? Do they provide hay? Do they clean stalls? These extras can soon add up. If you find a boarding barn you like, make sure it has room for your new horse before you arrive with him in the trailer.

Evaluating Your Horse Experience

Next, ask yourself, "Do I know enough about caring for a horse?" Have you ever actually looked after a horse by yourself? Even if you plan to board your horse, you still need to know how

Do you know what a horse eats?

to take care of him because the primary responsibility will always be yours. Do you know what or how much a horse eats every day? Would you be able to tell if your horse were sick?

If you don't know the answers to these basic horse-care questions, spend time reading some educational horse books. There are plenty of titles available at your local library. Borrow books from friends who ride. Ask your friends and family to buy you books for your birthday or holidays. The average bookstore doesn't carry a lot of horse titles (although the mega-stores do have a better selection); the best source for a more comprehensive selection is a large tack shop. Build your own library of equestrian titles. Good horse books are a valuable investment. You'll refer to them again and again.

Ask your friends which horse magazines they recommend, and subscribe to a couple. Most good magazines have practical articles that teach you how to look after a horse properly. They also have informative "Ask the Vet" type columns.

If you have a computer and a modem, you could subscribe to an on-line service. They have special chat rooms or bulletin boards through which you can communicate with other horse lovers. If you have a horsey question, post it on-line. You're sure to get a lot of replies.

Once you have some horse-care knowledge, you must consider your riding ability. Be honest. How experienced are you? If you have been riding for only a month or two, it's not really a great idea to buy a horse. Can you walk, trot, and canter a horse? Can you stop a horse if he spooks at something and bolts with you? Are you nervous or confident on a horse? If you're not sure about the answers to these questions, here are some ways you can learn more about horses without actually owning one first.

Riding-School Lessons

Before you even consider buying a horse, sign up for at least six months of riding lessons with a reputable instructor and make the most of your time there. Here's how:

Regular riding lessons increase your knowledge about horses.

- Arrive on time for your lessons and pay attention to your instructor. Ask questions if you don't understand. If your instructor is worth her salt, she won't mind explaining things to you.
- Take as many lessons as you can afford.
- Ride as many different horses as you can. You'll learn more and become a better rider if you can ride all sorts of horses.
- Arrive early and help groom and tack up the horses. These are technical skills you must have if you buy a horse.
- Once you have some experience, help the beginning riders mount, and lead them around the ring.

Arrive early for your lesson and help tack up a horse.

- Watch other lessons. Try to learn from what the other students are doing.
- Attend equestrian clinics (mounted or unmounted), seminars, or workshops offered by your riding school or neighboring schools.
- Volunteer to clean tack or feed the horses. Most instructors are happy for you to help. You may even get a few hours of free riding in exchange for your work.
- Make friends with other horse people. Offer to take care of a friend's horse if he or she goes out of town. Your help will be appreciated.

Once you have experience, give beginning riders a helping hand.

- Join a horse club. Many stables have dressage or combined training clubs. Enthusiasts hold meetings and show videos or invite guests to speak. Some clubs offer group trail rides.
- Volunteer to help at horse shows. You may be roped into setting up fences or manning the in-gate. Or you may get to assist the judge. Helping at a show prepares you for competing in the future.

Volunteer to Exercise a Horse

Once you've acquired the basic skills and confidence, hang a note on your barn's bulletin board or at a local tack shop offering

Volunteer to clean your tack after your lesson.

to exercise horses. Many people don't have the time to exercise their horses enough. Here's where you come in. An owner may want a reliable person to ride his or her horse once or twice a week. The owner will probably want to get to know you first and watch you ride the horse, but don't be insulted. You'll be just as cautious when others ride your precious horse.

You may have to sign a release form that states the owner is not responsible if you get injured while riding or working around the horse. On the flip side, you may ask him to sign a form that states you are not responsible if the horse gets hurt. If you come to an arrangement with an owner, go out of your way to be helpful.

Volunteer to exercise other people's horses for them.

Muck out or groom without being asked. Turn the horse out if he needs time out of his stall. Always return the horse to the owner in spotless condition.

Don't ask for money when offering to exercise horses unless you are a true-blue professional rider. Most owners are turned off by requests for payment. If you're like most horseless riders, the chance to ride and improve your skills should be payment enough.

Camp

Some riding schools offer riding camps in the summer for all ages. If you've got the spare time, sign up. You will probably get to ride once or twice a day and attend classes in horse management. You may be given instruction on equine nutrition, health, first aid, and breeding. You may also be assigned a horse to look after and ride as if he were your own. This is a great way to establish a special relationship with a horse.

Horse Vacations

If you've got the money and the time, go on a horse holiday. Begin by browsing through horse magazines to find travel companies that offer equestrian vacations. You could spend a week riding through the French countryside, jumping stone walls in Britain, or foxhunting in Ireland. Or you could herd cattle on a dude ranch in Montana. After spending days in the saddle, you'll be a better rider.

Talk to Horse Owners

Be friendly to riders who own horses. Ask for information that will help when you finally get a horse: Where do their horses live and how are they kept? Where do they buy their feed, and which farrier trims or shoes their horses' feet? How do they combine owning horses with a career? When do they find time to ride? Do they have a trainer, and how much do they pay for lessons? This information differs from area to area, so it's a good idea to find out about horse ownership where you live.

Leasing a Horse

If you'd like to give horse ownership a try without all of the responsibility, leasing may be the way to go. It's like renting a horse. Often an owner doesn't have time to ride her horse enough, or may be unable to pay the full boarding fee and would like some help. Leasing is usually beneficial to both parties. You agree to look after the horse for a set period of time, but the horse still belongs to the owner. You will probably be responsible for paying a portion—or all—of his feed, board, and shoeing, and possibly vet fees, too.

Leasing offers many choices. You can lease from a private owner or a trainer. If you pay the entire board, you'll have the horse to yourself all the time. If you pay half, you'll get to ride the horse only certain days a week. The owner may ride him on the other days with a half lease.

A trainer may want to lease a lesson horse to you because he's too frisky for other riders, but you get along with him just fine. Or the trainer may have too many horses to ride herself and would like you to take care of one of them for her. The money you pay for the lease may include lessons with the trainer.

Make sure the owner offers you a formal lease contract or arrangement before you take on the horse. A handshake is not enough. Things can go wrong, and you don't want to be stuck with a horse you can't ride. Have your riding instructor or a lawyer look carefully at the contract before you sign it. Do not lease a horse without getting satisfactory answers to the following questions:

- How long does the lease last?
- Where will the horse be kept?
- Are you the only person looking after and riding the horse?
- How many times a week are you able to ride the horse? Is an appointment or set time required?
- Does the horse come with tack and equipment, such as boots and blankets?

Find out where your leased horse will live.

- What can you do with the horse? Can you jump him or take him on trail rides? Can you take him to shows?
- Who is responsible for routine healthcare and maintenance, such as worming, regular checkups, and vaccinations? Who pays vet bills in an emergency?
- What happens if the horse is permanently injured and you cannot ride him anymore?
- Is the horse insured?
- Can you get out of the lease if the horse turns out to be unsafe or unsuitable for you? You don't want to get stuck making monthly payments for a badly behaved horse.

Who is responsible for the routine health maintenance, such as deworming, of your leased horse?

Lease agreements vary depending on needs of both parties. Here is sample language for a lease agreement which can be adapted for your use:

LEASE AGREEMENT

This agreement is entered into between _____, residing at _____, hereinafter referred to as "Lessor," and _____, residing at _____, hereinafter referred to as "Lessee."

A. Terms of Lease

This lease shall start on _____ and terminate on _____ for a period of _____ months and covers the horse described in paragraph B.

B. Description of Horse

a) Name: _____ b) Age: _____ c) Breed: _____

d) Sex: _____ e) Registration or brand number: _____

C. Payment Fee and Schedule

In consideration of this lease, Lessee agrees to pay Lessor the following sum(s) on the date(s) indicated below. (You may change this paragraph to suit your needs. Often a Lessor won't charge a fee. You will just be responsible for boarding, feeding, trimming, and shoeing the horse. This needs to be stated in writing.)_____

_____

D. Purpose

Lessee is leading said horse for _____

(Describe what you will be doing with the horse. For example, pleasure riding, showing, trail riding, etc.) and Lessee warrants that said horse is fit for said purpose(s).

E. Special Rights of Lessee

(This is where the Lessee must state any conditions he wants to put on the lease. For example, he may want only you to ride the horse or he may want the horse stabled at a particular facility during the lease.)

_____

_____

F. Special Instructions

(This is where the Lessee should list any special instructions for you. For example, the horse may need allergy medicine daily, specially formulated feed, or extra-thick blankets.)_____

_____

G. Risk of Loss

Lessee hereby assumes risk of loss or injury to said horse except where caused by negligence of the Lessor. Lessee agrees to purchase full horse mortality insurance on horse in amount of $ ____covering the terms of said lease and naming the Lessor as sole beneficiary.

H. Hold Harmless

Lessee hereby agrees to hold harmless from and against any and all claims, damages, liability, and expense in connection with loss of life, personal injury, and/or damage to property arising out of the use or care of the horse.

I. Ownership

Lessor warrants that he has good and clear title to said horse, free of liens.

J. Feed and Facilities

Lessee agrees to feed and stable the horse leased herein in accordance with the following instructions:

Stall: _____ (size and location)

Grain: _____ pounds per day _____ times per day

Pasture or turn-out: _____

Hay: _____ pounds per day _____ times per day

K. Care

Lessee agrees to maintain said horse in good health and to provide all necessary veterinarian and farrier needs at no cost to Lessor.

L. Liens

Lessee agrees to keep said horse free of all liens, encumbrances, charges, and claims, and Lessee agrees to hold Lessor harmless therefrom.

M. Default

Upon material breach of this Agreement by one party, the other party may terminate same. On any breach, the other party shall have the right to recover from said breaching party all reasonable attorney's fees and court costs.

This agreement is subject to the laws of the State of _____.

Executed this _____ day of _____, 200_, at _____ time.

Lessor

_____(name)

_____(address)

_____(phone)

Lessee

_____(name)

_____(address)

_____(phone)

The Search Begins

Once you've decided that you have enough time and money for a horse, and enough experience to be an owner, your search can begin. Often the best horses don't appear in advertisements because people who've heard about them by word of mouth quickly snap them up. Keep your ears open around the barn. It's a good idea to look for a well-known local horse because it's easy to investigate her temperament, health, and past performance.

Start by asking all the horsey people you know if they've heard of any good horses for sale. Your instructor or the owner of the riding school may know someone who wants a good home for a horse. If you know a horse veterinarian or a farrier, ask him or her, too. If you are a member of a local horse club, let other members know about your search.

Newspapers and Magazines

Local newspapers are a great place to find horses for sale. They are usually listed under livestock or horses in the Classified Advertisements. The best days to look are Friday, Saturday, and Sunday because savvy sellers know that people are likely to look at horses on the weekend, when they have plenty of time.

Look in free horse magazines, too. These are usually published monthly or biweekly, and are distributed at local tack shops. They often have a photo and description of each horse. Local publications are better than national ones because you won't have to travel too far to view a horse. National publications tend to advertise expensive horses for experienced professional and amateur riders. Most people don't have the resources to travel thousands of miles to see a horse. If you do decide to view a horse in another area or state, ask the owner to first send you a videotape of the horse. You don't want to waste time and money on travel if the horse is clearly not for you.

When you first scan the ads it may seem as though there are a lot of super horses for sale, but don't be fooled. People are not always as honest as they should be when describing a horse they're trying to sell. You have to read between the lines, so here are some terms and phrases you may come across. Let's look at the positive terms first:

- **Ideal first horse** or **Perfect for novice rider**: Well behaved, experienced, and a good mount for someone just learning to ride.
- **Bombproof**: Sensible, calm, and won't be scared by loud noises or unexpected happenings. If you're nervous in the saddle, this is the horse for you.
- **Well-mannered**: Obeys your commands. She won't barge around you, kick you, or knock you down trying to leap out of her stable.
- **Good all-around horse**: Performs fairly well in all horse disciplines—flatwork, jumping, and trail riding. She may be a good horse for children.
- **Honest**: Tries her best at all times and will do anything you ask her. She is not sneaky, stubborn, or timid.
- **Schoolmaster**: Very experienced and needs little instruction from her rider, whether she's being ridden on the flat or over fences.
- **Made**: Well trained and very experienced. Can be counted on to look after an inexperienced rider.
- **Ridden on the buckle**: So well-behaved and responsive that she can be ridden on a very loose rein.

An ideal first horse is calm and well-behaved.

- **Good to clip/shoe/catch/trailer**: Stands quietly when she is clipped or shod, is easily caught when out in the field, and steps into a horse trailer without any problems. Mild-mannered overall.
- **Imprinted**: Specially handled as a foal and is very used to humans.
- **Sound**: Not lame or ill.
- **Auto changes**: the horse can perform automatic flying lead changes, something that is important for a show horse.
- **Fancy**: A well bred, quality horse with good conformation.
- **Scopey**: jumps high fences with style.

A bombproof horse is unflappable in most situations and is ideal first horse.

A good first horse shouldn't mind being clipped.

Here are terms that you should avoid or investigate further:

- **Green horse:** Inexperienced and needs training.
- **Green broke:** Recently backed or ridden for the first time. If you haven't been riding long, it's not a good idea to buy a green or green-broke horse. When you're as inexperienced as your horse, you won't be able to train her properly and she will never reach her full potential. If you fall in love with a green horse, however, and can't stop yourself from buying her, sign up for lessons with a reputable trainer who can help both of you every step of the way. You will have to learn together.
- **Not a novice ride:** Needs an experienced rider. The horse may be extra strong or extremely temperamental, and probably not for you. Pass her by.
- **Potential working hunter/show jumper:** Young or inexperienced and needs a lot of training. If you've never

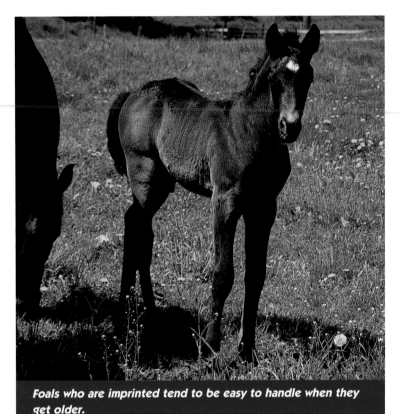

Foals who are imprinted tend to be easy to handle when they get older.

trained a horse yourself, you may want to pass. But if she seems talented and you really like her personality, talk to your trainer. She or he may encourage you to buy the horse and then offer to work with both of you in the future.

- **Lively, spirited, needs a confident rider:** Steer clear. The horse is probably hard to control. Lively and spirited can also mean flighty and headstrong. These are not desirable characteristics in a first horse. And even if you consider yourself a confident rider now, an obnoxious, dangerous horse can reduce you to a nervous wreck and make you regret the decision to take her home.

If you buy a green horse, it's a good idea to get help from a trainer.

Abbreviations

As you read horse ads, you may come across a few confusing abbreviations. Sellers often use them to fit in more information about the horse. Here are some common ones:

AA—Anglo Arab
A/O—Amateur Owner
DWB—Dutch Warmblood
Han—Hanoverian
HH—Hands High (measurement)
O/F—Over fences (meaning jumping)
QH—Quarter Horse

SWB—Swedish warmblood
TB—Thoroughbred
Trak—Trakehner
TWH—Tennessee Walking Horse
WB—Warmblood
X—Cross (for example, Welsh-X)

Tack Shop Bulletin Boards

Most tack or feed shops have bulletin boards where sellers post signs about horses for sale. You need to visit these stores at least once a week to stay ahead of the game. If a horse catches your eye, ask the staff members if they know her. They may be able to give you some information.

Riding Schools

If you fall in love with the horse you ride during lessons, it can't hurt to ask if the owner would be willing to sell her. Riding school favorites can make excellent first horses because most are calm, obedient, and unflappable. They are used to inexperienced riders. Plus, you already know the horse and get along with her, and your instructor should be familiar with her too. Don't expect a school horse to be cheap, though. If the horse is good, the school will part with her only for what she's worth. Be prepared to negotiate a more attractive price.

Before you hand over a check, ride the horse outside of her normal arena. Lesson horses often act different when they're taken out of the ring and ridden away from other horses because they are not used to the new environment. School her in another ring by herself to see how she behaves, and take her on a trail or two. Horses who plod slowly and safely around the riding school ring day after day may suddenly become raving loonies when they're on an exciting trail ride in open countryside.

Check your local tack shop bulletin board for horse ads.

Dealers

Dealers buy and sell horses for a living. If you go to a dealer, he or she will ask what sort of horse you're looking for and then search for one who fits the description. Dealers charge for the service of finding you a horse and/or take a commission from the seller of the horse.

A dealer usually has many horse contacts. Once you describe what you want, the dealer starts calling around to see if any of his or her contacts have a horse who might suit you. A dealer may also have a barn full of horses for sale. People often send their horses

If you buy a lesson horse, take her out of the arena and on a trail ride first.

to dealers to be sold. The horses are trained (or retrained) and prepared for sale to the general public.

Ask your instructor if she knows a dealer in your area with a
good reputation. This is important because there are some ques-
tionable dealers around who, at first glance, might seem reputable.
Ask horse owners at the barn if they've heard of an honest dealer
who sells quality horses. Truly honest dealers do not sell terrible
horses because it might hurt their reputation. They offer to buy
back a horse if she turns out to be unsuitable. They should want
to make their customers happy. If a dealer has a horse for you,
arrange a convenient meeting and be on time. A reputable dealer

acts like a professional businessperson and has a tidy barn. There should be a ring where a buyer can try out a horse properly.

If you like a horse, a good dealer lets you try her a second time and should be happy to let a vet perform a pre-purchase exam. Don't trust pushy dealers who try to pressure you into buying a horse you are not sure you want. Bad dealers have plenty of ways to encourage you to buy a horse. They may tell you that they've had several offers on the horse, or that they are going to show her to several other people. Be strong and walk away from a bad dealer. Buy only when you are ready.

Auctions

Going to an auction to buy a first horse is asking for trouble. You know very little about the horses that are for sale, and unless you are really experienced (or a veterinarian), it is very difficult to establish a horse's age or judge how healthy she is. In addition, most auctions have very small rings. You probably won't get to ride the horse or see her move properly before she goes on the auction block.

Be suspicious at an auction. There may be a very good reason the horse has not been sold privately. She may be ill, lame, or have a behavioral problem that the owners don't want anyone to know about. At the more dubious auction houses, you may see neglected or injured animals who will break your heart and if you decide to bid on one, you may find that you are bidding against someone from the horse-meat industry. Auctions such as these can be upsetting. If you are a sensitive person, stay away.

Occasionally, there are auctions at which you can buy a decent horse. You need to ask horse people in your area to recommend a reputable auction house. Young, unbroken horses with special breeding are often sold at special "Performance Sales," and youngsters lacking the speed to be successful on the racetrack are sold at

Thoroughbred auctions. You might find a bargain or two, but probably only if you are an experienced horse person. Most of the Thoroughbreds need retraining before they can be riding horses.

Finally, don't expect a bargain at an auction. Auctioneers want people to get excited so that, in a frenzied crowd, they will spend more than they would if they were purchasing the horse privately. Also remember that most sales are final at an auction. If you buy a real monster, you won't get your money back.

Rescue Groups

If there is an equine charity based in your area, inquire whether it has an adoption program. There are horse charities all over the country dedicated to helping injured or neglected horses, and many have rescue groups that take in horses who have been removed from bad situations. Once the horses are nursed back to health, they may be put up for adoption. Most organizations are very particular about who adopts their horses, and charity workers often inspect a prospective adopter's home to make sure the adopter can look after a horse properly. If you adopt a horse, it is likely she will remain the property of the charity, which may check on her regularly to make sure she is healthy and happy.

Adopting a horse from a charity may seem like a good idea, but you need to get to know the horse before you take her home, so spend some time with her at the rescue center. Rescued horses don't always make terrific first horses because they may have been abused in the past and afraid of humans. They may kick, bite, and generally be unfriendly. They may also have health problems because of past neglect. Think carefully before adopting a rescued horse.

Want Ads

Putting a "horse wanted" ad in a local newspaper or horse magazine is an inexpensive way of letting others know that you're searching for a horse. A cheaper way is to put the ad on bulletin boards at local barns, riding schools, and tack shops. Write the ad carefully. State the age, size, and type of horse you would like. Be honest about how much money you want to spend, and note how far you will travel to view a horse. Write that you can offer a great home to the perfect horse. Describe yourself and the sort of riding you intend to do. Perhaps a person who is thinking about selling her horse, but hasn't placed an ad yet, might see your ad and call you.

Place a classified ad so the perfect horse finds you.

What Kind of Horse is Right for You?

Before you look at horses, think carefully about what sort of horse you need. If you're taking lessons, ask your instructor what kind of horse she would recommend for you. Consider what activities you're going to do with your new horse. If you ride English and want to jump hunter courses, don't waste your time looking at a quarter horse who is an expert barrel racer. If you want to ride in western pleasure classes and go trail riding, bypass the high-stepping warmblood who wins dressage classes. Your search will be less complicated (and less stressful) if you have a good idea about the age, size, breed, and type that suits you.

Age

A good first horse is usually in the nine- to fourteen-year-old range. Many people automatically think they should look only at young horses, but this is not a great idea. Older, experienced mounts make the best first horses. A horse over eight years old should know the ropes and be able to give you a lot of confidence. He probably knows how to walk, trot, and canter on command. He may have been taught to jump. He is likely to have been on a trail ride or two, and he may be calmer in a stressful situation than a younger horse.

A young horse needs a lot of training, and if you're inexperienced, he may take advantage of you and pick up some bad habits such as bolting off or grabbing at grass. He may not know basic skills such as halting on cue or picking up the correct leads at the canter. And think twice about buying an unbroken two or three year old, even if he is a bargain. He'll have to be broken to the saddle and bridle, and backed, or ridden for the first time, so he will require a great deal of time and training. Besides that, you can't ride such a young horse seriously until he is three or four because his bones are still developing, and too much work can strain them and damage their growth. Only an experienced rider or a novice with an attentive trainer should consider buying a horse under seven years old. Of course, there are exceptions to every rule. If you are fortunate, you may find the best-behaved, smartest five year old in the world. Sometimes it all comes down to luck.

Horses live well into their twenties, so a horse in his teens will probably be around for a while. If you look at horses older than seventeen, inquire about their general health. Older horses may have special dietary needs and can suffer from arthritis, just like humans. But if well-cared for, an older horse can live a very useful life and excel at his job. There are plenty of active older horses.

Size

If you've been riding a while, you probably have a good idea about what size horse you need. Ask your instructor for her opinion too. Remember that horses are measured in hands. A hand is 4 inches. The height of a horse is found by taking the measurement of a straight line from the ground to the highest point of the withers, which are at the base of the neck. You can measure a horse by using a special wooden measuring stick, but if you don't have one and want a rough estimate, rest a crop on the withers, and then with a measuring tape, measure from the crop to the ground.

Horses are measured from the withers at the base of the neck.

Look for a horse or pony in proportion to your size. This is absolutely essential if you plan to show the horse because a judge notes how well you fit him and vice versa. When sitting astride a horse, your legs should reach at least halfway down his sides.

If you're a small person, you might consider buying a large pony for your first horse. In general terms, a pony is a horse standing 14.2 hands or under. Many ponies are strong and sturdy, and can easily carry an adult. If you're petite, you don't need a huge horse because you probably won't be strong enough to control him at all times. You may not be able to stop

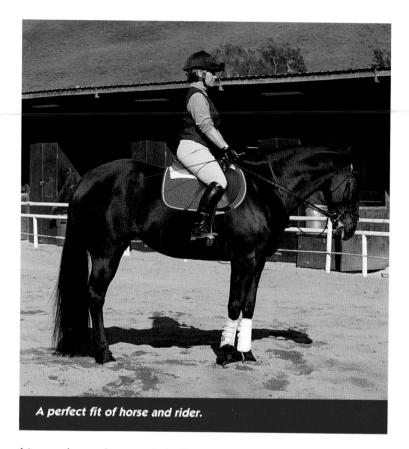

A perfect fit of horse and rider.

him, and your legs won't be long enough to use on him properly. If you try out a big horse, make sure you can mount him on your own, without a leg up or a mounting block. You won't always have help.

You don't want a horse that is too small either. If you're too tall for a particular horse, not only do you look awkward but the horse may not be able to perform properly because you unbalance him. If you are too heavy, you could give a horse back problems. If you are a large (but fit) person, look for a big, muscular horse. There are plenty of horses out there that can carry your weight.

If your horse is very tall, he must have good ground manners so you can handle him.

Sex

Every horse person has an opinion on what gender of horse they prefer. Many people feel geldings (neutered males) are easier to handle and less moody than mares (females). Some equestrians swear that mares can be flighty and unpredictable. The truth is that there are good and bad horses of both sexes. You need to judge each horse individually.

Some mares can be a bit sensitive when they are in season (ready to mate), but this sort of behavior lasts only a few days a month, usually during the summer. They may be a bit touchy when you

Breeding a mare can be expensive, and risky, for an amateur owner.

handle them and act aggressively toward other horses. Still, there are many mares in season who get on with the job at hand, and you may not be able to tell their condition. Some riders swear by mares. They claim they are sharper and have more spark than geldings in competitive situations.

If you hope one day to breed a foal of your own, you obviously need a mare. Breeding a mare is a complicated business for an amateur owner, and you can't really be sure what kind of foal you will get. There are far too many horses already, and many end up in slaughterhouses. Do you really need to add to the overpopulation of horses in this country?

If you are new to the sport of riding, steer clear of stallions—male horses who have not been gelded. Stallions can be unpredictable and aggressive and are not allowed at some boarding barns and shows. Often a stallion is more interested in being friendly to the mares around him than in doing his work.

Personality

A horse's personality is one of the most important factors to take into consideration before you hand over any money. Even if the horse is extremely talented, you won't enjoy being around him

A friendly personality is an important quality in a first horse.

if he tries to kick or bite every time you enter his stable. And don't think you'll be able to miraculously change his personality. An older horse, particularly, is unlikely to alter his ways. Your goal should be to buy a horse that is good-tempered, friendly, calm, and sensible.

When you meet a horse for the first time, he should have his ears forward and be interested in you. You should be able to pat him and walk around him without his pinning his ears back, throwing his head around, grinding his teeth, and looking at you in a threatening manner. Avoid buying a horse that behaves nervously, and steer clear of aggressive bullies who charge at you or knock you over when you're in their way. You should not dread handling your horse. Owning a horse should be a pleasant experience.

Price

The more talented and experienced a horse is, the more expensive he will be. A horse who has won a lot of ribbons competitively costs more than one who has been ridden only for fun on trail rides. The old adage *you get what you pay for* is often true when it comes to negotiating price. Prices can vary from area to area as well. You might consider driving a short distance to another county or neighboring state to get a better price. Talk to your instructor or other horsey friends and find out how much a suitable all-around horse should cost in your area, and stick to that price range while you're searching for your new horse.

As a rule, a younger, unbroken horse costs far less than a "made" horse, but you won't enjoy your bargain if you don't know how to train him properly, so consider your skills first. Horses tend to be more expensive in the seven- to twelve-year-old range. Prices start to go down again after a horse turns thirteen or fourteen. A well-trained showing star can cost thousands of dollars. A top-class show pony can fetch more than $20,000 in today's market. A talented reining horse can cost $30,000. A dressage star competing in upper-level competitions can set you back

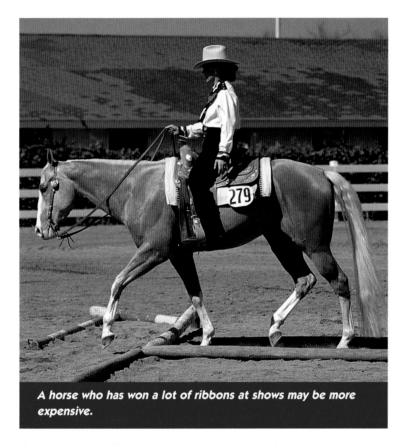

A horse who has won a lot of ribbons at shows may be more expensive.

$50,000. And what about an international show jumper? You'll have to shell out $100,000 or more! Consider your price limit before you begin your search. If you know your budget in advance, you can weed out candidates that are far beyond the reach of your wallet.

Before you faint and give up your search, take heart. There are plenty of good, moderately priced horses, and you are sure to find one in or around your price range. If you look carefully, you should be able to pick up a solid riding horse, suitable for an amateur owner, for under $10,000. Many are in the $3,000–5,000 range. If you get lucky, you may pay far less than that.

Remember, decide how much you can spend and stick to your guns. You might have to be patient and look at quite a few horses, but you'll be glad you did when you find one who suits your needs, fits your skill level, and doesn't bankrupt you.

Color

Color should not influence your choice. If a horse is well behaved and has a pleasant personality, his color should not be important. There's no point in owning a stunning pinto if he bucks you off every time you ride. And while you might dream of buying a beautiful palomino, it's not very clever to pass up a perfectly decent bay horse.

You probably know what a bay or palomino horse looks like, but when scanning the horse ads you may notice a few uncommon colors. Western riders often call chestnut horses "sorrel." Buckskin, a yellow-brown color is often called "dun" by English riders. Here are some other examples of coat colors:

- **roan**: black or brown body with a significant amount of white hairs interspersed
- **dapple gray**: a light gray coat covered with rings of dark gray hairs
- **flea-bitten gray**: brown specks of hair on a gray coat
- **liver chestnut**: a very dark shade of chestnut
- **tobianos and Overos**: different types of pinto patterns
- **strawberry roan**: chestnut body with white hairs interspersed
- **steel or iron gray**: a dark gray

There are some people who have color biases. For example, they claim that chestnut mares tend to be moody and difficult, but this can be true of any color horse. Color does not dictate personality. Ignore the old wives' tales and buy the horse who is the right one for you.

Gray horses require a lot of grooming to keep them looking clean.

Some horses are harder to keep clean and care for than others, but it is easier to take care of a stain or two than deal with a serious behavior problem.

For example, grays and pintos show dirt easily, can be sensitive to sunlight, and may suffer from sunburn in the summer. You may have to slather sunblock on delicate areas such as their noses and faces every day or they could burn and develop painful sores and scabs. Older gray horses are also prone to developing melanomas (tumors) around their rectal area, under their tails. These growths are usually harmless, but they are unsightly so you might want to ask your vet if they can be removed surgically.

If you want to compete in show jumping, buy an experienced horse.

What You Plan to Do with Your Horse

Before you begin your search, decide what equestrian activities you want to do, and then look for a horse who fits the bill. If you are one of those people who likes to ride both English and western, there are quite a few multitalented horses who can be ridden both ways.

Ask the owner to tell you the different things the horse can do, and have the owner demonstrate them if she can. If the horse is a good one, the owner will love bragging about him.

You need to be honest about your riding ability too. How experienced are you? If you're just learning how to jump, do you need to try out a top-notch show jumper? No. Find a horse who suits your riding level or is already competing at your showing level or just a little bit above. Ask the owner what sort of classes the horse competes in. If they're the sort of classes you'd like to enter in the next year, go see the horse.

Which Breed is Right for You?

As you read the advertisements for horses in your area, you will notice that most of them include the breed of the horse. Horse shoppers usually have a general idea about what sort of breed they're searching for, and they look for ads with breed descriptions. What kind of breed would you like to buy? If you've been riding for a while, you probably have a favorite breed or two, but it's a good idea to keep an open mind about breeds when looking for a first riding horse. You may have your heart set on buying a flashy Arabian when a quiet quarter horse would suit you better.

A purebred horse, one with both parents of the same breed, can sometimes be costly because reputable breeders strive to match high-quality mares and stallions. Mixed breeds (sometimes called "grade horses") have parents of two different breeds or unknown breeding, and usually cost less than purebred horses.

If you're interested in a particular breed, contact the breed association or registry (see Resources for addresses) and request an informational packet about the breed. The association can also put you in touch with breeders or trainers in your area who might know of horses for sale.

If you decide to buy a purebred horse, it's very important that the seller provide you with some documentation or a certificate stating the horse's breeding. The certificate should come from a legitimate breed association and state the name of the horse's dam (mother), sire (father), and the name of the breeder or farm where the foal was bred. When you buy the horse, these registration papers should be signed over to you.

If you completely fall in love with a breed, by all means go out and look at horses of that breed. If you are lucky, you will find one who suits you. You can then become a member of the breed association and research your horse's pedigree. You can show the horse at special breed shows as well as enter breed classes at open shows. Plus, you'll meet people who also share a love for the breed. But while a horse's breeding might be very important to a professional rider or trainer, you shouldn't give it too much thought. If a horse seems perfect for you in every other way—and the price is right—don't worry about a fancy birth certificate.

American Quarter Horse

The American quarter horse is the most popular—and populous—breed in America. It can be ridden both western and English. If you're interested in western roping, reining, barrel racing, trail riding, and pleasure riding, the talented quarter horse is for you.

Originating in the seventeenth century, quarter horses were first bred by English settlers in Virginia and the Carolinas. The settlers crossed quick-witted Native American ponies of Spanish ancestry with English Thoroughbreds. The colonists soon noticed that their new horses were very fast over short distances, so they began organizing races of a quarter mile. By weekday, the horses would work in the fields, and on weekends they would dash down dirt tracks and main streets. These speedy horses became known as the "Celebrated American Quarter Running Horse," but the name was eventually shortened to quarter horse.

The quarter horse proved strong enough to carry heavy riders all day, and as cattle ranches spread across the West the breed became a popular mount for cowboys. The quarter horse is known for its "cow sense"—an innate talent for rounding up cows and "cutting," or singling out, animals from their herds. If you are looking at quarter horses, you may notice that a few of them have brands, usually located on their hindquarters. These are ranch brands and they tell you where the horse lived and worked before you found her. You may be able to find out more about your horse's background by researching the brand. Call the Bureau of Livestock Identification in Sacramento, California, to find out more information on a particular brand (see Resources).

Because quarter horses often carry a substantial amount of Thoroughbred blood in their breeding, they are also good English mounts and often very competitive in working hunter and jumper classes. And if you're looking for a good family horse, quarter horses can be ridden by children or adults because they are famous for their sensible personalities and calm dispositions. They have muscular hindquarters and strong, sound legs. Most stand between 15 and 16hh (hands high). They come in solid coat colors, including bay, chestnut, gray, black, or dun, and may have white markings on their heads or legs.

If you buy a quarter horse, you can join the American Quarter Horse Association. It has plenty of activities for lovers of the breed, and every year it holds its Quarter Horse World Championship Show, a huge multi-day show in Oklahoma City that attracts thousands of enthusiasts and horses from around the country.

Thoroughbred

If you specialize in English riding, dressage, show jumping, or eventing with your horse, consider buying a Thoroughbred. Graceful, refined, and intelligent, these horses tend to be long-legged, angular, and lean. They range in size from 15 to 17hh and usually come in solid colors—such as gray, bay, black, and chestnut. Some have white markings on their faces and legs.

Hundreds of thousands of Thoroughbreds are bred for racing each year.

Because they are fast, Thoroughbreds are used for racing. Hundreds of thousands of them are bred for the track each year, and since few become superstars, many end up as riding horses and adapt quite well to their new jobs. Not every Thoroughbred has been raced, but it's easy to find out if one has seen a track or two in her lifetime by simply looking in her mouth. If she has a number tattooed on the inside of her upper lip, it's likely she has raced or been in training. Pay attention to her legs, which may sport lumps and bumps. Racing as a two or three year old puts a tremendous strain on a youngster's long legs, and the horse may never recover and become fully sound. Only a veterinarian is able to tell if there has been serious damage. If you aren't experienced, don't buy a young horse off the track. It may take years of retraining before she becomes a reliable riding horse.

A purebred Thoroughbred is not always the best choice for a first horse. Some are high-strung and sensitive. They may spook easily and be difficult to stop. It is often a better idea to look for a Thoroughbred-cross. For example, a sensible Thoroughbred/quarter horse–cross may suit you better.

Arabian

If you want to do endurance (long distance) riding, an Arabian may be the perfect horse for you. Watching an endurance ride, you'll notice that most of the competitors are riding Arabians or Arabian-crosses. These horses are nimble, quick, and have a lot of stamina.

The Arabian breed dates back to 2500 B.C. These horses were prized by Bedouins, nomadic people who live in the Arabian Desert. The Bedouins treated their horses like royalty because legend says they believed that their god, Allah, created the breed from "a handful of wind." The horses lived in luxurious tents with people and were often fed by hand. Foals were weaned very early, and the Bedouin children fed them camel milk and helped raise them. Breed enthusiasts believe this early interaction between humans

Arabians are extremely intelligent and sensitive.

and Arabians is the reason they are so friendly. They are very curious and will approach strangers with interest. They can also be very playful.

Arabians are used for western riding, dressage, and jumping. Occasionally, they are spotted in English jumper competitions but are not often seen in hunter classes. Judges generally place Thoroughbred-type horses over Arabians in open hunter classes, but there are plenty of Arabian breed shows. Some competitions even have elaborate costume classes in which owners dress up like Arab sheiks or princesses in honor of their horses' heritage.

The Arabian is a small breed, so if you are petite, it might be the one for you. The horses usually range between 14 and 15hh, and come in solid coat colors such as chestnut, bay, gray, or black. Like their Thoroughbred cousins, they may be too high-spirited for someone new to riding, but there is no reason why a part-bred Arabian wouldn't make a terrific first horse. Quarter horses and Morgans are often crossed with Arabians and produce nice riding horses.

Morgan

All Morgans are descended from a strong little stallion named Figure, who lived in the late 1700s. Figure was renown around his home in Vermont because of his speed and great strength. The 14hh stallion was bred to many local mares, and the offspring became known as Morgans.

Today, Morgans are very popular. They are known for their easy dispositions and their willingness to please. They are small, ranging from 14.1 to 15.2hh and have short backs, strong necks, and muscular hindquarters. Their basic colors are bay, brown, black, and chestnut, although other colors are found.

Morgans have a high-stepping action, which is popular with people who want to ride saddle-seat-style or drive their horses. They are versatile and can be ridden western or English, and can even be found jumping or eventing. Many Morgans today find that

Morgans are high-stepping, spirited horses.

dressage is ideal for them, because of their upright conformation and their springy, energetic movement.

Appaloosa

Many people fall in love with Appaloosas because of their eye-catching spots. They come in a variety of coat markings. Appys are used for everything: western riding, eventing, show jumping, hunting, and dressage. Because of their coloring, they make very popular parade horses. But even though they may be flashy, they are sensible horses. In fact, they are great all-round riding horses.

Appaloosas are flashy looking but sensible.

Appaloosas were originally bred by the Nez Perce tribe of the Pacific Southwest. They tend to be stocky, muscular, and hardy. They have tough hooves, strong legs, and powerful hindquarters. They range in height from 14.2 to 15.2hh. Appaloosas tend to have thin manes and tails. Their eyes look a bit different from those of other horses because of the white sclera that surrounds the eye.

If you decide that you simply must have an Appy, ask the seller if the horse has spots before you visit. Because they can have quite a bit of quarter horse blood, a few Appaloosas are solid-colored, and this may reduce their value to you.

Paint horses are likely to catch a judge's eye.

American Paint Horse

If you watch horses in a parade, you are bound to see a paint or two in the bunch. Paints stand out because of their flashy markings. Their coats usually consist of white splashes mixed with another color, for example, brown, black, or gold.

The paint breed originated with pinto marked horses that came to America with Spanish explorers. Some were traded or stolen by native tribes, while others got loose and joined wild bands. Eventually, paint horses became prized by cattlemen working the western plains. Today's paints have to bear certain bloodlines and characteristics to be considered purebred.

Paints tend to be muscular and stocky, yet their heads and necks are often refined, similar to that of Thoroughbreds. Most stand about 15 to 16hh. For a horse to be eligible for the American Paint Horse Association, the horse must come from stock registered with the American Paint Horse Association, The American Quarter Horse Association, or The Jockey Club (Thoroughbreds), as well as meet a minimum color (spots) requirement.

Paint horses are ridden in hunt-seat classes and occasionally are seen in jumper competitions. But paints are mainly ridden by western enthusiasts who love to ride them in pleasure and reining classes. Because they look so spectacular, they're bound to catch the judge's eye.

Tennessee Walking Horse

If you are interested in doing a lot of trail riding, you might consider buying a Tennessee walking horse. This southern breed is famous for its "running walk"— a smooth, comfortable gait that covers a lot of ground. It also has a smooth canter, which is often called the "rocking chair gait." Many people who ride gaited horses, such as Tennessee walkers and saddlebreds, swear that they are the most comfortable horses to ride. If you have hip or back prob-

Tennessee walkers have a unique, ground-covering gait.

lems or arthritis but still want to ride, these may be the perfect breeds for you.

Tennessee walkers are usually ridden saddle-seat or western, and are often seen displaying their high-stepping leg action at horse shows. They are also used to work cattle and for carriage or buggy driving. They come in solid colors, pinto patterns, and may have white markings on their legs and faces. Their stature is around 15 to 16hh.

You may have seen the exaggerated high step of the Tennessee walker show horse. This horse's gait is enhanced through the use of platforms on its front feet and "action devices"—chains. The walking horse has been the subject of cruelty in the form of "soring," where the horse's feet and legs are made sore in order to get them to step higher. The government, and in turn, the breed association, has taken action to try to stop unscrupulous competitors from soring horses. Today, flat shod and "versatility" classes are becoming more popular to show of the Tennessee walker's many true talents.

American Saddlebred

Like the Tennessee walker, the saddlebred is another high-stepping horse developed in the American South. Saddlebreds are a multitalented breed that can be ridden western, driven in harness, jumped over fences, and competed in dressage. They are excellent trail horses, and because of their size (usually 15 to 16.1hh), they can carry a tall adult all day.

There are two types of saddlebred. The three-gaited saddlebred walks, trots, and canters with high-leg action but in a slow, collected manner. A five-gaited saddlebred has two extra paces: the slow gait, which is a bouncy, prancing pace; and the rack, a spectacular high-stepping, speedy gait that is often seen in show classes. Saddlebreds come in a lot of colors, but bays and chestnuts are the most common.

Saddlebreds are known for being flashy show horses.

Warmblood

If you're experienced and very serious about dressage or show jumping, think of buying a warmblood. The term warmblood is generic and usually refers to a group of large, strong horse breeds that originated in Europe. Here are some warmblood breeds you might come across while scanning the horse ads: Swiss, Dutch, Danish, and Swedish warmbloods, Trakehners, holsteiners, and Hanoverians.

Warmbloods are usually huge, ranging in size from 16 to 18hh. They are almost always solid-colored and can have white

Warmbloods make top-class dressage horses.

markings on their faces or legs. If you see a horse who has a brand on her thigh muscle, she is probably a warmblood. Each of the breed associations has its own symbol, so you can tell what kind of horse the horse is by checking out the brand.

Because of their careful breeding and the fact that many of them were imported from Europe, warmbloods are often very expensive and out of the price range of the first-time buyer.

Cross-Breed

When you're looking for the perfect first horse, don't overlook any suitable grade horses, also known as cross-breed horses. Some of the best and most well-behaved riding horses around are cross-breeds. They are often less flighty and more sensible than their purebred counterparts.

Often they are hardy and if fed properly can live happily outdoors year-round. Most cross-breeds have the ability to grow warm, shaggy coats and can stay out in winter unless it gets extremely cold. They tend to have fewer health problems than purebred horses too. If you don't have a lot of money to spend, you'll probably find that a cross-breed horse is less expensive than a purebred one.

Some popular crosses include: quarter horse/Thoroughbred; quarter horse/Arab; Morgan/Arab; and Appaloosa/Thoroughbred. Sometimes a talented pony breed blends well with a larger horse breed. For example, the Irish Connemara pony crossed with a Thoroughbred often results in a small, athletic horse with plenty of jump in her.

If you find a horse you like but can't find out anything about her breeding, don't give her mysterious background a second thought. Is a piece of paper listing a fancy bloodline really that important? If a horse is friendly and obedient and does her work without a fuss, it doesn't matter who her parents were, and you could save a lot of money.

A lovable cross-breed may suit you the best.

Finding a Horse

When you spot an ad or hear about a horse who seems right for you, act quickly! If the horse sounds good to you, he's going to sound good to other people as well. You want to be one of the first people to see the horse because it often takes more than one visit to make a decision. But before you jump into your car with your riding boots, call the seller and ask her some detailed questions. The horse may seem wonderful in the ad, but sadly, sellers aren't always honest. You don't want to drive three hours or more only to discover that he's totally wrong for you.

Get on the Phone

By now you should have a good idea about the sort of horse you want. The first phone call you make to the seller is the best time to learn if her horse fits the bill. Here is a list of questions that will help you get a clear picture of the horse:

- What is the horse's breed?
- How old is the horse? Seven to fourteen years is good for a first horse.
- How big is the horse? A horse must be proportionate to your size.
- How much is the seller asking for the horse? Sometimes ads do not state a price.
- How long has the seller owned the horse and why is she selling him? If she has owned him for only a couple of

months, be suspicious. The horse could be badly behaved or dangerous or have a medical problem. Besides that, the seller could actually be a dealer, not a private owner. Dealers tend to keep horses only a short time. Then you need to ask yourself, "Why is a dealer, not the owner, selling this horse?"

- How long has the horse been for sale? If a horse is talented and well behaved, he will be snapped up quickly, so if he has been on the market for a couple of months, ask why. There may be a good reason. For instance, a horse may be re-advertised due to "time-wasters," people who said they were going to buy the horse and then backed out.

- What does the horse do well? Does he enjoy jumping or is he a dressage star? If you want to enter western pleasure classes, a high-strung show jumper is not for you. A good first horse should be an all-around horse, one who does a bit of everything.

- What has the horse been used for in the past year? Has he been to any shows or gone on any trail rides? Has he been doing an activity that you plan to do too? If he hasn't been ridden in a year, he may have to be retrained.

- What kind of personality does the horse have? You want a pleasant, friendly horse.

- Does the horse have any antisocial habits, such as kicking or bucking?

- Does he have any stable vices? These are nervous behaviors that a horse does in his stable or pasture when he is bored. Unfortunately, they mainly stem from domestication of the horse. The two most common stable vices are cribbing and weaving. Cribbing means that the horse chews on wood in his stall or on fences. It can damage his teeth, and swallowing wood can cause colic, a serious equine stomachache. Unfortunately, once a horse develops this annoying habit, it's almost impossible to stop it. Weaving is when a horse stands in his stall, swinging his head from side

Does the horse have a pleasant personality?

to side. It is a comfort mechanism, similar to a human sucking his or her thumb, and may indicate that the horse is upset or bored.

If a horse is really talented, you may decide you can live with these vices. You may find, however, that some barns do not let you board a cribber or weaver because the managers feel the behavior will be picked up by surrounding horses. Recent equine behavior studies have shown that these vices are not necessarily copied from one horse to another, but still many people prefer to isolate cribbers and weavers, which may make the problem worse.

A horse who cribs has to wear a special collar to prevent him from chewing on things.

- Is the horse healthy and sound (not lame)? An owner should be able to tell you if the horse has a medical condition or has ever been injured. There are some medical conditions with which you can live. For example, some horses with white face markings have sensitive skin and burn easily. This you can control by putting sunscreen on their faces. But don't waste your time viewing a horse who has serious health issues such as recurring bouts of laminitis, a blood disorder that affects the hooves. Or if he has navicular disease, a degenerative hoof disease, you should not buy him because he may be lame frequently. Find out if the horse has ever had colic. If he has recurrent bouts of this equine stomachache, he may have digestive disorders that could affect his health. If you don't know how serious a condition is call up the equine vet who will care for your future horse and ask him about it. He should be happy to answer your questions.

Don't get discouraged if you hear the horse was injured in the past. At least the owner is being honest with you. Some injuries heal perfectly well and don't affect the horse's performance. Don't reject a horse just because he has a scar or two, either.

Here are some things not to do when talking to a seller:

- Don't waste your time or the seller's. If the horse sounds unsuitable at the beginning of the conversation, don't ask the rest of the questions. Say "no thank you," and hang up.
- Don't tell the seller how much you are willing to pay for the horse. This can be discussed after you have seen the horse.
- Don't exaggerate your riding ability. This can be dangerous. Be truthful and let the seller know what sort of riding you do and at what level. If she is honest, she will tell you if the horse is not right for you.

The Visit

If the horse sounds wonderful, arrange to view him. Fix a day and time and get detailed directions from the seller. Horse people often live in remote places, and you don't want to get lost.

Then ask your riding instructor or a horsey friend to come along. It's very important to get a second opinion on the horse. You can't very well watch yourself ride, and it always helps to have an outside opinion. Do offer to pay your instructor for her time.

If you have access to a video camera, bring it along and have your companion tape you as you ride. Study the video later—it could help you decide if you want to make an offer or not.

Always arrive on time when viewing a horse; first impressions are important. The seller should be friendly and the barn area neat and tidy. If the place looks run-down and messy, the horse might be in the same condition.

The horse should be in his stall or paddock or out in a field, not tacked up. If he is, be suspicious. If he has been ridden already, ask for how long. If the horse is high-spirited or badly behaved, the seller may have lunged him or ridden him to tire him out before you mount him. Some disreputable sellers have even been known to drug a horse with sedatives so he is quiet when ridden. Beware! If you are not vigilant, you may end up with a horse who behaves quite differently at home.

The horse should be groomed and clean. If he is covered in mud, it is difficult to tell what he looks like. A caring owner wants her horse to look good for potential purchasers. The horse should look healthy and well fed. His coat should shine, and his eyes should be bright. He should have been recently shod so that he is sound when ridden by prospective buyers.

Signs of a Suitable Horse

You should be able to figure out pretty quickly what kind of personality the horse has. It will be obvious to you when you walk

The horse should be waiting for you when you arrive at the barn.

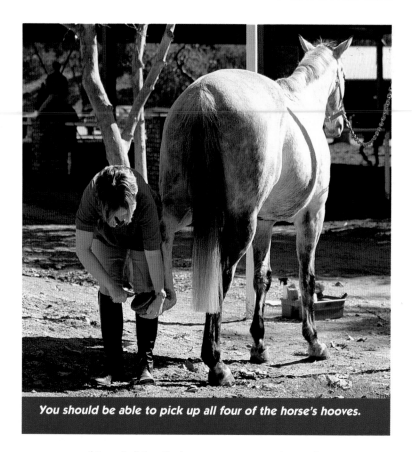

You should be able to pick up all four of the horse's hooves.

up to meet him. A friendly horse appears curious about you. He leans forward and gives you a good sniff with his ears forward.

A suitable horse lets you catch him and put a halter on him with no fuss. It is absolutely essential that a horse be caught easily. Chasing a horse around a pasture for an hour is extremely frustrating. If the horse is in a stable or tied up, ask the owner if she has any problems catching him.

Once the horse is tied up, he should stand quietly. You should be able to pat him on his neck, shoulders, and back, and he shouldn't mind if you walk behind him. He should also let you pick up all four hooves.

Signs of an Unsuitable Horse

If the horse acts scared of you out in the field and won't let you catch him, be wary. If he shakes his head and makes it difficult for you to put his halter on, take note. An unsuitable horse is irritable or suspicious around you. He may pin his ears back in an aggressive manner, and may fidget when you try to pick up his hooves. He may shy away from you, which could indicate a general fear of humans. A horse who has not been looked after properly is skinny and clearly looks unhealthy. You may be able to see his ribs. His coat is dull and shaggy. He may not have much energy.

Conformation

If the horse is friendly, check his conformation. Conformation is the way a horse is put together and the way he looks. Obviously, some horses are prettier than others, but very few horses have perfect conformation. You have probably noticed a horse at your barn with a long back or legs that seem crooked. Things like this are conformation defects or faults. If you are planning to show or compete, look for the best conformation possible.

Some defects are signs of physical weakness and may affect the horse's ability to walk, trot, canter, or jump. If a horse has square, club feet, for example, they may affect the way he moves, and he will probably win less than a horse with more rounded hooves. Other defects may affect his health. For example, a horse with a "parrot mouth"—a severe overbite—will not be able to eat properly, and it may be difficult to keep weight on him. Other kinds of poor conformation affect only the way a horse looks. Big ears won't stop a horse jumping a 4-foot fence. If a fault doesn't affect his performance in any way, you really shouldn't worry about it.

Now, nobody expects you to be as capable of spotting minute defects as a vet is, but if you've been riding for a while, you should be able to spot some glaring problems—defects that should make you think twice about buying the horse. Here are a few things to look at:

Legs: Look at them from the front, side, and back. All four legs should be nice and straight. His front legs should not be knock-kneed, which means his knees bend inward. Nor should they be pigeon-toed, which means his hooves point inward. If his back legs bend in at the hocks, he is "cow-hocked." If they bend out at the hocks, he is "bow-legged." These faults could (but may not) affect the way the horse moves. His knees should be broad and flat and not stick out too much.

Run your hand down all four legs. Do you feel any big lumps or bumps? Is the horse sensitive to your touch? If he has a few lumps or scars, ask the owner how he got them. Bumps can often

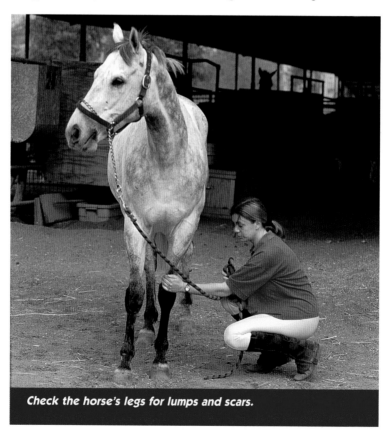

Check the horse's legs for lumps and scars.

be splints, bony growths on the leg caused by too much work at an early age. Most splints don't cause problems but occasionally one will make a horse lame. Get a vet to look at them before you hand over any money.

Hocks: Sometimes a hock is slightly enlarged and a bit squishy to the touch. This is known as a capped hock, and it isn't usually serious. Often this is caused by stress and strain on the back legs when a horse gets up after lying down. If a hock is huge, a vet needs to look at it.

Hooves: All four hooves should be about the same shape and size—round, not square and boxy. They should not have large cracks or rough edges. You may not be able to ride a horse who has a large crack in his hoof because the crack will get bigger if he moves a lot. His pasterns should have a nice slope from fetlock to hoof. Upright pasterns are prone to cause lameness, or at the very least an uncomfortable ride.

Pick up his feet and look at the shoes. If they are a funny shape, or if you have never seen shoes like them before, they may be corrective shoes that help to fix a hoof weakness or leg problem. Ask the seller why the horse has unusual shoes.

Chest: Look at the horse from the front. He should have sufficient room in between his front legs to move easily. If he has a really narrow chest, his front legs could rub together and cause sores.

Back: Run your hand along his back. It should dip slightly in the middle, but not too much. If it dips a lot, he has a swayback—a particular problem with old horses—and it may be hard to find a saddle that fits him properly or comfortably for him. If the horse has a really long back, he could suffer back problems. If his back is too short, he may have a short, choppy stride that makes him uncomfortable to ride.

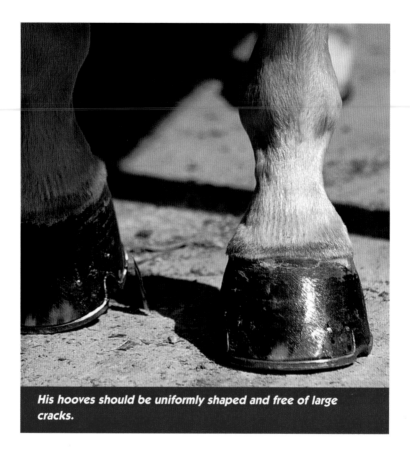

His hooves should be uniformly shaped and free of large cracks.

Withers: The horse's withers—the bony base of the neck where the mane ends—should rise up from the back to the neck, with a decent amount of muscle on each side. They should not stick up much because it will be hard to find a saddle that fits. You may have to buy a specially made saddle that goes around the withers.

Questions, Questions, and More Questions

Don't be shy about asking the seller a lot of questions. You want all the facts before you make such an important decision as buying a horse. There are a few more things you might want to check.

Have a snoop in the horse's stall or corral. What sort of bedding is on the floor? Is it one of the most common types of bedding such as straw or wood or cedar shavings? If the stall floor is covered in something unusual such as shredded paper, ask why. Straw can be dusty and may aggravate a horse's allergies. Sensitive horses may need special dust-free bedding such as paper. You should think twice before buying a horse with a breathing problem or an allergy because he requires special care and may be difficult to keep fit.

Find out what kind of food the horse eats. Does he have a special diet? Is it hard to keep weight on him? If you have a busy schedule, you may not want to drive all over the place to buy spe-

Does the horse have any conditions, such as allergies, that might make horse-keeping complicated?

Does the horse need a special diet?

cial feed for a picky eater. Plus, some special foods and hays can be expensive and your bills will increase.

Will the horse load into a trailer without a fuss? If you plan to show your horse, you don't want to get into a fight with him every time he has to get in a trailer. A good first horse should happily walk into a trailer. If the seller has a trailer, ask her to lead the horse into it while you watch.

If, after looking at the horse from head to hoof, you decide he is not the horse for you, let the seller know, say "thank you" to the seller and leave. Don't waste her time or yours by continuing the conversation. Chalk the visit up to experience. Every time you look at a horse you add to your equestrian knowledge. Viewing a lot of horses helps you decide what sort you really want. You may see plenty of horses that you don't want. Be patient. It may take some time and quite a bit of investigative research before you find a suitable horse. That's okay. The more savvy you become, the more likely you are to buy a decent horse.

Trying Out a Horse

If you like the look and personality of a horse, it's time to get to know her better. After watching the owner work with the horse on the ground, ask if you can do a few things with her by yourself before you ride her.

Handling the Horse

It's a good idea to handle the horse before riding her. You will probably have to work with her all by yourself once you get her home, so see how she behaves. Here are a few things you can do to get to know the horse.

Lead her around in her halter with a lead rope. If she has a chain over her nose, which is used to keep her under control, ask the owner if you can take it off. If she's going to be your first horse, she shouldn't require a chain. She should walk next to you calmly and slowly, and halt when asked. If she pulls you around, barges in front of you, or refuses to move at all, she has bad manners and probably doesn't respect her human handlers very much. A horse such as this will need a lot of retraining. If the horse tries to grab at grass, don't worry too much. Simply pull her head up, and ask her to move on again. Most horses sneak a snack if allowed, so don't hold it against her. It won't be hard to break this habit.

Tie her with a lead rope. She should stand fairly still. It's not a good sign if she won't tie or pulls back and tries to break the rope. Once again, a horse who won't tie will need some retraining. Can you work with her yourself or will you need some help from a trainer? Find out if she ground ties—stands still with the untied lead rope lying on the ground. Ground tying can be useful on trails.

Ask if you can groom the horse and pick out her hooves. She should stand quietly, not try to nip or kick as you work around her, and she should let you pick up her feet without a fuss. This is a good time to ask the owner if the horse minds being clipped. If you plan to show her, you may have to clip her at some point, and you may want to trim her legs, bridle path, or muzzle whiskers with clippers even if you don't show her. Some horses hate being clipped and get very hard to handle when they hear the clippers buzzing. They often have to be tranquilized beforehand.

Ask if the horse lunges, which is circling the handler at all gaits on a long line. If she does, ask the seller to lunge her for a few minutes. This gives you a chance to see how she behaves on the lunge line. It also gives you a terrific opportunity to see how she moves without a rider hindering her. Watch her walk, trot, and canter in both directions, and try to videotape her in action. Lunging also warms up the horse before you ride her and can get rid of a little excess energy if she is feeling frisky.

Tacking Up

Offer to help the seller tack up the horse. Pay attention to the tack because it gives you clues about the horse's personality. A good, safe, first horse (for western or English riding) should wear a simple snaffle bridle and a plain noseband. If the horse is going to be ridden English, a standing martingale (one that attaches to the noseband) is acceptable, but steer clear of a horse who wears a severe bit such as a gag, or a bit with a sharp, twisted mouthpiece. These bits let you know that she is probably quite strong and difficult to stop at times.

Check out the noseband too. If the horse wears a figure-eight noseband or a severe Kineton, she is probably a puller and will open her mouth to evade the bit. Look for other gadgets too, such

Offer to tack up the horse yourself to see how she behaves.

as side reins or training devices. Gadgets such as these are only quick-fix options for a horse with a behavior problem. They aren't permanent solutions. A first horse in particular shouldn't need all these extras. Your trainer or horse friend should be able to spot extra-strong bits or nosebands and point them out to you.

Observe the Horse Being Ridden

Even though you may be eager to mount the horse, ask the seller to ride her before you do. If she won't, be suspicious. Why won't she ride her? It's okay if she has arranged to have someone

Ask the seller to ride the horse first while you watch.

else ride her in front of you. It is important for you to get an idea of the horse's behavior with another rider before you get on.

While the other person is riding the horse, note whether the rider is wearing spurs or carrying a crop. Is the horse so sluggish that the rider needs to use them constantly? Imagine yourself on the horse's back. Would you want to be hitting and kicking her as much as this rider is? If the horse is extremely grumpy and stubborn, she might not be the right horse for you, although you won't be sure until you get on. You may ride her better than the other person. When it is your turn, first try her without spurs and the crop, and then use them only if you need to.

Does the horse look calm and move forward happily?

When the rider mounts, does the horse move around? It is very aggravating to own a horse who won't stand still when being mounted. Think what a problem it would be trying to remount out on a trail. A horse should always stand still on a fairly loose rein for mounting.

At the walk, the horse should be happy to move forward on a loose rein. She should not prance around or try to trot. The rider should not have to keep a tight hold on the rein. The horse should look calm and fairly relaxed because she is being ridden in familiar surroundings.

At the trot, the rider may shorten the reins a bit. The horse should trot right away. The rider should not have to kick, kick, and kick. Once they get going, is the rider bouncing high out of the saddle? If so, this might mean the horse is really bumpy at the trot. The horse should move along steadily. She should not zip around at top speed, nor should she plod along at a snail's pace. If she is going to be ridden western, she should jog slowly on a loose rein and her head should be fairly low.

The horse should pick up the canter, or lope, quickly and move forward at a steady pace. She should pick up the correct lead. If she is young, she may not pick up the correct lead right away, so if you buy her, be prepared to spend time training her to canter with the inside leg leading. The horse should not drag her nose along

Watch her jump a fence or two.

the ground and pull the reins out of the rider's hand, nor should she gallop about with her head held high.

If you ride English and plan to jump, ask the rider to clear a few fences. The horse should jump over a few small fences at the trot, and then one or two at the canter. Does she rush her fences, zooming along with her head in the air, or does she approach them calmly? The fences don't have to be gigantic, just about the size you want her to jump should you buy her.

If you feel nervous about getting on the horse after watching someone ride her, or you just don't think she is the horse for you, say "thank you" and leave. There's no use riding a horse you don't like, or one who scares you. The horse might act up and hurt you. There are plenty of good horses out there, so don't risk your life trying ones who are badly behaved.

But if you like the horse, it's time for you to try her. If you have a choice, ask to ride her in an enclosed arena first. She might get excited in a big field and run off with you. See how you get on with her in a ring before riding out in the open.

Your Turn to Ride

Put on your safety helmet. Even if you don't like to wear a helmet, you should wear one when you ride a strange horse. Next, adjust the stirrups to fit, and check the girth. Then mount the horse without any help. At home you may have a mounting block or a friend who gives you a leg up, but there may be times when you won't have assistance. It's important that the horse stand still so you can mount easily.

Walk the horse around the ring several times. Give yourself time to get comfy in the saddle, and get organized before you ask for a faster gait. See how much pressure it takes on the reins to get her to turn. If you ride western, see if she knows how to neck rein. Then trot or jog her in both directions and do a few circles. Ask her to halt from the trot or jog to make sure you can stop her

Does the horse stand quietly while you mount?

quickly. Does she listen to your commands? Does she move away from your leg, or do you have to really kick her to get her to move?

Once you are sure you can stop the horse, try a canter or lope. Don't worry too much if she doesn't pick up the correct lead at first. After all, you've never ridden her before, and you don't know the cues that make her do her work correctly. If you don't get the lead, ask the seller how she gets it and try again. A good horse won't mind if you get things wrong at first, and she shouldn't get upset if you make a mistake or two. If she gets riled up and misbehaves at the slightest error, she's probably not the horse for you.

Trot or jog the horse in both directions around the ring.

When you have her cantering or loping, does she continue steadily around the ring or does she slow into a trot or jog the second you take your leg off her? Some of the best first horses are a bit lazy, but you don't want to have to beat a horse to get her to move. On the flip side, does she bolt forward into the air the instant you squeeze her? Don't buy a horse who is ultra-sensitive and overreacts to every cue.

If the horse runs off with you and you have a difficult time stopping her, pass her by. A horse who pulls a lot or runs off with her rider is not safe, and it's very important that you be in control at all times. If you can't stop her quickly, you will be a menace to yourself and others on trails and around the barn—and you could get hurt.

The Horse's Specialty

If the owner tells you that the horse is good at doing something, such as rollbacks or flying lead changes, try the moves yourself, if you feel confident. Be proud if you get the horse to do what she is supposed to do. After all, you've never ridden her before. If you plan to barrel race or do trail classes with her, lope around a barrel or two and open and shut a gate. Back her up a few steps. Practice a few moves you might do in a reining class. If you don't get the move at first, stop, get organized, then try again. Your trainer may suggest a few things for you to do too.

If you plan to jump the horse, ask your friend or trainer to set up a few fences in the arena. If you're a new rider, don't go crazy and set up 4-foot fences. Stick to heights of 2'6" to 2'9". Raise your stirrups a hole or two so you can get into jumping position easily. Start with a cross-pole fence and trot over it. Make sure you steer her right into the middle of the fence. Jump the same fence several times at the trot and then at the canter before you try another one.

How does the horse jump? Does she rush the fence with her head in the air? If she does, don't buy her. She'll knock down more fences than she'll leave up. Is she comfortable to jump? Do you feel happy jumping her or do you feel scared? If there are several fences in the arena, ask your trainer to set up a small course of four or five jumps. The horse should jump them at a fairly steady speed. If she is green, she may not jump as nicely as a more experienced horse, but you should be able to tell if she is willing and enthusiastic about jumping.

Don't get annoyed or embarrassed if the horse refuses a fence or two, or if she knocks down a fence. You are bound to make a few mistakes and the horse isn't used to you. In fact, she doesn't know you at all. But be wary if she runs out or refuses at almost every fence and then knocks the rest down. Perhaps this is not the horse for you.

See how the horse behaves on a quick trail ride.

Trail-Ride Test

If you plan to take your new horse on trail rides, it's a good idea to see how she acts outside the arena. Ask the seller if there are any short trails you can go on or a big field you can ride in. Failing that, ride her all around the barn area. Note how she behaves around cars. If she becomes a quivering wreck at the sight of a truck, she might not be a terrific trail horse. Ideally, the seller should tack up another horse and accompany you on the ride. If she won't or can't, maybe your trainer or friend could walk beside you on the trail.

Ask the seller if the horse walks through water. Many horses are afraid of water because they cannot perceive its depth, and it may take a lot of training to get them to enter creeks or rivers. If there is a creek or small stream around, ask if you can walk the horse through it. If she hesitates for a few seconds, but eventually walks in, it's likely she'll improve with time and practice. But if she backs up and is naughty, you may want to pass on her. It could take professional training to get her into water.

If you're riding a young horse, she may spook at a few things. A log on the ground might be a scary monster! Don't worry too much about this. As long as the spooking is not too violent and she doesn't throw you completely out of the saddle, you should be able to work on this when you take her home. Most horses adapt to trail riding after a while, especially if you take them out regularly with a calm, experienced trail horse. Horses learn a great deal from each other, good and bad.

Decision Time

If you're not interested in the horse, tell the seller you don't think the horse is for you, wish her the best of luck with the sale, and leave. If you are interested in the horse, don't make an offer right away. Tell the seller you need a few minutes in private to discuss the

What do you think? Do you like the horse?

horse with your friend or trainer. The seller should not be listening. Ask yourself how you feel about the horse. If the video camera has a viewer, rewind the film and take a look at yourself riding her. Ask your friend or trainer for his or her opinion.

If you're still unsure about the horse, don't rush. Tell the seller you need some time to think about the horse and review your options. You will be in touch. It might be necessary for you to arrange a second visit and ride, but remember, unless the seller absolutely loves you and wants her horse to go to you, she may very well sell her to someone else while you are making up your mind. If you're not absolutely sure you want her, however, this is a risk you should take.

A few sellers let you take the horse home on a trial basis for a week or so. Trials can be risky, though. You have to have a contract stating the responsibilities of each party before taking a horse on trial. For example, you may be responsible for vet bills if the horse injures herself or gets sick.

If you're willing to take a chance on the horse, make an offer. If the horse is fairly decent, don't insult the seller by offering a really low price. She probably won't take it and may stick to her original asking price with a vengeance. Most sellers will bargain a bit, but if they are asking a fair price in the ad, you should expect them to go down only a couple hundred dollars. Horse people have a pretty good idea what a horse is worth.

If you think the horse is extremely overpriced once you've met her, tactfully explain why you think so to the owner. She may come down over the next few days if she realizes no one else is going to pay such a high amount. However, if the horse is very well-behaved and talented, and the seller has several people interested in the horse, she will probably demand the full price.

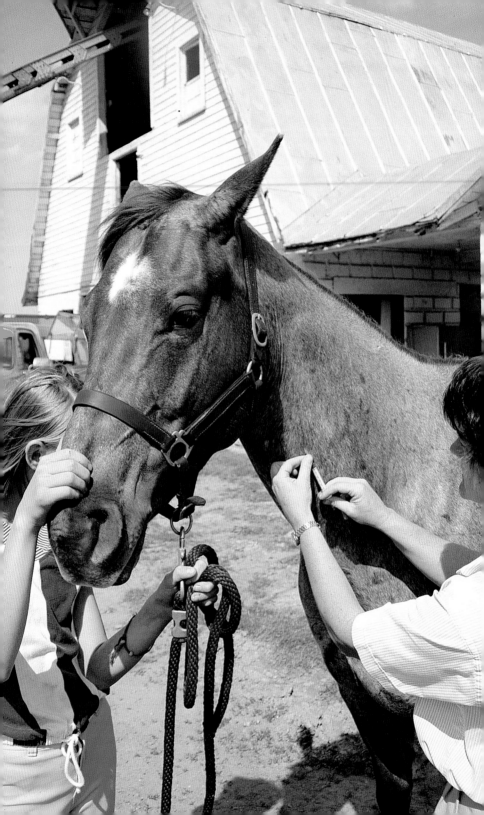

7

The Veterinary Pre-Purchase Exam

Once you've decided a horse is definitely for you, have him checked by a veterinarian before you hand over any money—unless you feel very confident about your knowledge of horses. Some folks think they are experienced enough to spot something wrong with a horse and skip the vet exam, or if the horse is very inexpensive, they might decide it's not worth spending what could amount to several hundred dollars on a vet exam. But paying a vet now may save you money later. If you can afford it, have an exam done. A vet might discover that the horse is lame, has a respiratory problem, or suffers some other serious defect. A small bump on the horse's leg could turn out to be a serious splint that could make him lame. A runny nose could mean the horse has an allergy that could prevent him from breathing properly and affect his work.

No reputable seller will ever object to a pre-purchase veterinarian's exam, but she may want you to put down a deposit on the horse first. This is common. Write a contract stating that you are paying a deposit for the seller to hold the horse for you until after the exam, and that the deposit will be returned if the horse fails the exam. The contract might also specify that you are obligated to hand over the cash if the horse passes. (The seller won't be very happy if you suddenly decide you don't want the horse anymore.)

Usually, the buyer arranges the vet exam. Most people think it's a bad idea to have the horse's regular vet do it because the buyer should get an independent opinion. If you don't know an equine vet, ask your trainer, another horsey person, or the manager of a local barn to recommend one. Then arrange a time when the vet can come out and examine the horse. The seller should be present during the exam, and it should be held in daylight hours so the vet can get a good look at the horse.

Exam Day

You should be present during the pre-purchase exam. It will probably take an hour and a half. Bring riding clothes in case the vet asks you to ride the horse. The horse should be groomed, wearing a halter, and waiting for the vet. Before the exam starts, the vet will probably ask you what you plan to do with the horse and will consider your plans while he or she does the exam. A horse who is expected to do top-level eventing will be examined slightly different from one who is going to be used for quiet trail rides through the woods.

Here are some of the things a vet checks or does during a pre-purchase exam:

Teeth

The vet is able to tell approximately how old the horse is by looking at his teeth. Unfortunately some sellers may tell you a horse is younger than he really is, or they may be unsure about his age. A vet can be quite accurate if the horse is under nine years old. It is difficult to be precise if the horse is older than nine, but the vet should be close to the correct age.

The vet also checks to see if the horse's teeth are in tip-top condition. A horse should have his teeth rasped (filed down) at least once a year, but not every seller is conscientious about this. If

The vet may rasp the horse's teeth during the pre-purchase exam.

the teeth are too long or sharp, the horse may have eating problems, and won't keep weight on easily. A metal bit might be painful in his mouth. The vet might go ahead and rasp the teeth if they need attention.

Eyes

The vet looks at the horse's eyes with a special instrument called an ophthalmoscope. This has a small light beam on it that the vet shines into the horse's eyes. Usually, the vet takes the horse into a dark area, inside a stall, for example, to see the inside of the eye better. He or she looks for cloudiness or discoloration, which

The vet checks the eyes for signs of cataracts.

could mean the horse has a cataract—an eye ailment that usually affects older horses. Cataracts get worse with time and can make a horse blind. You shouldn't buy a horse with cataracts because his vision will almost certainly weaken.

Nose and Throat

The vet looks down the horse's throat and up his nose to make sure they're clean and free of obstructions such as tumors or other growths. If the nose is runny, the vet will try to find out why. The horse could have an infection or be allergic to something.

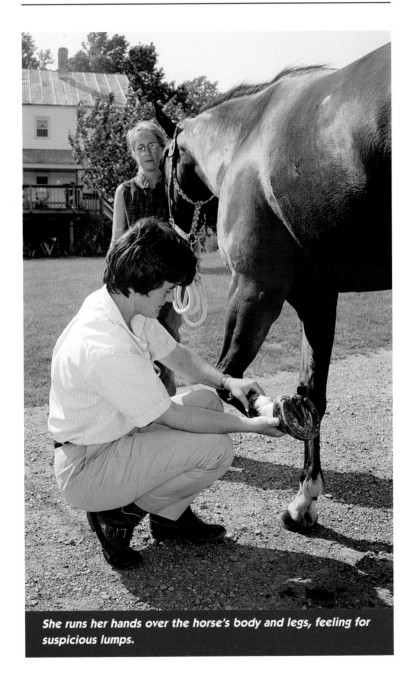

She runs her hands over the horse's body and legs, feeling for suspicious lumps.

Ears

The vet checks the horse's ears to make sure they are clean. Lice, mites, and small bugs often make their home in a horse's ears and can irritate their equine host. A horse with mites or lice in his ears may shake his head frequently or rub his ears on anything he can—including you!

Lumps and Bumps

The vet runs his or her hands all over the horse's body and legs, searching for swellings, lumps, or scars. The vet may be able to tell if the horse has been injured in the past. He or she may also know if a lump or bump is a serious flaw.

Heart and Lungs

The vet listens to the horse's heartbeat and his lungs with a stethoscope while the horse is standing quietly. The vet can tell if

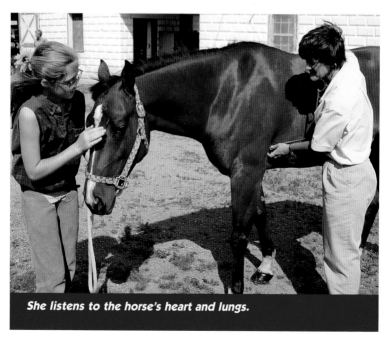

She listens to the horse's heart and lungs.

the heart is beating normally and whether the horse's lungs are clear or filled with fluid, which make it hard for him to breathe easily.

Next, the vet asks someone (probably the seller) to lunge or ride the horse at a trot and canter for a few minutes. The vet pays attention to the way the horse sounds as he moves forward. If his breathing is raspy and heavy, he may have lung problems. When the horse is halted, the vet listens to his lungs and heart again noting how long it takes for the horse's breathing to slow down after hard exercise. This is called the recovery rate. The vet knows how long it should take for the horse's heart rate to get back to normal, which is usually thirty to thirty-eight beats per minute.

Legs

Lunging is a great way for the vet to spot leg problems or lameness. Afterward, the vet checks each leg carefully to see if the knee and hock joints are flexible. He or she picks out the hooves

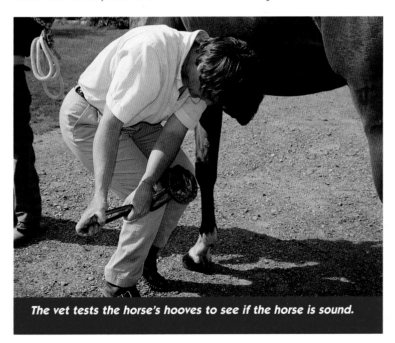

The vet tests the horse's hooves to see if the horse is sound.

She does a flexion test to help her spot lameness.

to get a close look at the frog and the hoof wall. The vet then asks someone to trot the horse away from him or her and then back again so the vet can see how the horse moves from the front and the back.

Then the vet performs a flexion test by lifting up a horse's leg as high as he or she can for about thirty seconds, letting it down, and watching again while someone trots the horse away from her quickly. If the horse has a major problem trotting after a few steps, he may have joint trouble and become lame in the future.

Blood Tests

Some vets do blood tests, which means they draw blood from the horse and take the sample back to the lab so it can be analyzed. Blood tests show if the horse has any dangerous viruses that might spread to other horses. They also conclude whether the horse has been drugged recently or is on any medications or dubious supplements that you

The vet watches the horse trot away from her looking for signs of soreness.

should know about before buying him. Blood tests can take a few days, so be prepared to wait before you can take the horse home.

X-rays

X-rays raise the price of the pre-purchase exam, so many people skip them. But if there is serious doubt about the soundness of the horse's legs, it is important that all four be filmed. The vet probably has a portable X-ray machine that produces a film in a few minutes. He is able to spot weaknesses that could cause lameness.

The Examination Form

During the inspection, the vet fills in an examination form with the horse's age and coat markings for identification purposes. When the vet has completed the form, he or she will tell you if the horse has passed or failed the examination. If the horse passes, you

A veterinary pre-purchase exam can be money well spent.

can buy him. But don't think that because a horse passes the vet exam that he's 100 percent perfect in every way. The vet is judging only the horse's physical state on a particular day. He could go lame two days after you buy him—that's life with a horse. A passing certificate is no guarantee that he will be healthy for years to come either. Unless the vet makes a huge mistake, it's unlikely that you'll get any compensation from him or her if the horse turns out to have a problem that wasn't obvious during the exam. And the seller is just as unlikely to give back your money once you've taken ownership.

If the horse fails the exam, ask why. He may have a serious problem that will prevent you from doing what you want with him. If you want to use him for show jumping, for example, and the vet finds severe splints, he or she probably will not pass him. You still have to pay the vet for the exam. If the defect is pretty severe, it is best to be hard-hearted and look for another horse. If you have a contract, the seller should return your deposit.

The vet may tell you the horse has a problem that can be managed with special care or that he will never be completely healthy but will be suitable for the sort of riding you have in mind. In this case, you must decide if you are willing to live with the problem and buy him anyway. What might be a big problem for someone else might not be so serious to you. For example, a horse with dust allergies in the stable might do fine if you keep him in a grassy field all of the time.

If you think you can live with the horse's problem(s), you might be able to negotiate the price with the seller—if it is clear that the horse never will pass a pre-purchase exam. A horse who fails pre-purchase exams is not easy to sell.

Home Sweet Home

After you've agreed on a price with the seller, find out how she wants to be paid. Some sellers accept only cash, which can be inconvenient for you. Others ask for a banker's draft or certified bank check—a check, which cannot bounce, that you pay your bank to write for you with the seller's name on it. If the seller knows you, she may accept a personal check, but don't count on it. Discuss these arrangements before you collect the horse.

A conscientious seller provides you with a bill of sale. Just in case she doesn't, make a copy of the bill of sale at the end of this chapter and use it when you hand over the money.

This is also a good time to ask about the horse's daily routine, her schedule for worming and shoeing, and what she eats. Knowing her regular schedule and sticking to it at her new home will make her move less stressful.

Where's the Horse Going to Live?

Now that you've decided to buy the horse, where's she going to live? Ideally, you should have a place picked out before you start your search. If you're lucky enough to have horse property or live on a farm, you'll just bring her home. Otherwise, you'll have to find somewhere decent to keep your new purchase.

If you don't know very much about the horse facilities in your area, look in the yellow pages under "Horses" or "Stables." Go to your local tack shop and check out the bulletin board for boarding facility advertisements, and ask the shop's employees if they can recommend someplace.

When looking at the barn ads, it's important to pay attention to the facility's location. It should not be far away from your home, school, or place of work. You should be able to visit your horse every day, and this will be difficult if the barn is too far away. Try to keep her within twenty miles or less. You want to be able to nip out and see her on your lunch hour or before work. You must also be able to get to her quickly if there's an emergency. If you're like most horse folk, you are too busy to waste precious time simply sitting in a car.

Here are some places you could keep your new horse:

A Riding School

If you're taking lessons already, your instructor may encourage you to keep your horse at her riding school. Riding schools often

A riding school is a great place to keep your first horse.

have private horses on the premises, and this can be a great move for the first-time owner. Your instructor can keep an eye on you and your horse and help you as you need it. She can continue to give you regular lessons, and if she's a good instructor, she'll teach you how to look after your horse properly.

There are a lot of people with whom you can ride and you may make some new friends. Some riding schools have excellent facilities, and you might be able to use the arenas and jumps.

If you're very busy with work or other responsibilities, consider letting the school use your horse for lessons several times a week. Your boarding fees will be reduced and your horse will get some extra exercise. You should have a formal agreement that covers how often your horse is going to be used and who is responsible financially if she gets hurt or injures someone. If you don't trust your instructor, or the riding-school management, don't let your horse be ridden by anyone else. Some schools may take advantage of your not being around and use your horse too much or put unsuitable riders on her.

A Boarding Facility

A boarding facility is a farm or ranch—usually with stables, pens, or fields—where you can keep your horse for a fee. Most have a manager or owner and workers who feed your horse every day. If your horse is stabled, she will probably be brought in at night, turned out in the mornings, and blanketed if necessary. Your horse's stable may be mucked out too. Each barn has its own regime. Make sure you like the way things are done at a stable before you bring your horse there, and look for a facility that suits your style of riding. Some specialize in dressage, others in western reining. If you're interested in hitting the trails, you want a barn that is close to a park or some other wide-open space.

The rates at boarding facilities vary by area. Generally, you get what you pay for. A barn with fantastic facilities, such as an indoor arena or a cross-country jumping course, can be very pricey. There

Your horse may have her own stall at a boarding barn.

are four typical types of board: field, pen, stable, or "do-it-yourself." Field board is generally the cheapest as it requires very little work. Your horse stays out in a field or pasture all of the time and is fed outside. Pens are also relatively inexpensive. They vary in size but usually accommodate one horse and are partially covered. Some barns have "in-and-outs," which are stables with a small pen attached so the horse can go in and out as she likes. If your horse is a thin-skinned purebred, she needs to be stabled—at least at night. This increases your boarding fee.

Some barns charge you a lump sum for feed, stable bedding, mucking out, and turning out. This is usually called "full board," but the barn may still bill you extra for services such as putting on blankets, grooming, or feeding additional hay. This can nickel and dime you to death, so investigate all extra charges before you choose a home for your horse. "Partial board" means that you will shoulder some of the responsibility of caring for your horse; for instance, you may buy her hay and feed.

If you are a hands-on person and have some spare time, see if you can find a "do-it-yourself" barn. This means you look after your horse yourself. You pay minimal rent for the stable and field, and then you feed, muck out, and turn out your horse. You'll buy the bedding and feed yourself. If you luck into a stable with other knowledgeable owners, you can work out rotations and share the work.

Your House

If you want to keep your horse at home, first check with your local authorities to find out if your property is zoned for horses. Zoning regulations vary from area to area, and from lot to lot, depending on the lot's size. You don't want to move your horse in, only to find out she needs to leave the next day.

You must also have the proper facilities for a horse. If you have a field, it must have a strong fence made of wood or a synthetic material. Never use barbed wire—it can severely injure a

You'll save money by looking after your horse yourself.

horse. Walk around the field and check for breaks in the fence before you turn the horse out.

The field should have a constant supply of fresh water and some shade for hot days. Trees—or a purpose-made shelter—will keep a horse cool. Some sort of field shelter, or a stable, is also needed in case the horse gets ill or injured and needs to be confined. If you plan to keep your horse in a pen, she must have plenty of room to turn around and lie down.

Finally, your horse should have some equine company. Horses are gregarious by nature and very few truly like being alone. Some actually get depressed when left alone for long periods of time and develop behavioral problems. If you have the room, try to find another responsible horse owner to share your field. You can help each other with the work, you'll have another pair of eyes checking on your horse, and you will be able to go away, occasionally. You could also offer a home to a

Your horse needs equine company if she is going to live at your home.

retired horse or pony. Ideally, there should be one acre per horse, but check what your city or county horse-keeping ordinance allows. Many West Coast properties have small backyard paddocks that can be home to several horses.

Transportation

You'll have to transport your horse on moving day. If you've never driven a trailer before, this isn't the time to start. Ask an experienced friend to move the horse, or see if your instructor knows of someone who transports horses professionally. Be prepared to pay the driver.

Have a full hay net ready to put in the trailer so your horse has something to nibble on during the trip home. Borrow or buy padded shipping boots to protect your new horse's legs in the trailer, and take along a halter and lead rope too.

Bring travel boots to protect your horse's legs in the trailer.

Put a hay net in the trailer so your new horse can eat on the trip home.

Insurance

Consider taking out an insurance policy on your horse before you pick her up. After all, the minute you hand over that check she becomes yours. She could injure herself two seconds after she gets in the trailer, and you could be stuck with a big bill. Equestrian insurance policies can cover the death or illness of your horse. They can also cover injuries and any damage your horse may do to herself or others. Study insurance ads in horse magazines and find out what different policies cover, and then compare the cost with your investment in your horse. How much can you afford to lose?

Handing over the Money

When you arrive at the barn with a trailer, your future horse should be groomed and waiting for you. After you pay for her, the seller should give you a signed receipt stating that you have paid her for the horse and you are the owner. Many people use a bill of sale for this purpose. We've enclosed one at the end of the chapter that you can copy and fill out on sale day. Both you and the seller should keep a signed copy.

If the horse is a purebred, the seller should also sign over the registration papers to you. As the new owner, you must reregister the horse under your name with the breed association. The seller should also give you the horse's veterinary records so you can tell if her vaccinations are current.

Finally, it's a good idea to let the seller load the horse into the trailer. She is used to her former owner and she might not follow you in. Be patient. You can unload her at home.

Welcome Home

When you arrive at your home or barn, unload the horse and take off her protective boots. Walk her around so she can take in

Buy horse insurance if you will be doing risky activities such as cross-country jumping.

It takes a few days for your horse to get used to her new pasture companions.

all the sights. She might be a bit excited at first, so keep her away from other horses. Now is a good time to worm her too, just in case she is infected with any parasites.

If she is going to be living in a field with other horses, don't just toss her out with the others. This can be very stressful. If you can, keep her separated from the others for a few days until she settles in. Horses in herds have a strict hierarchy, or pecking order. There is usually a boss—or alpha—horse who gets fed first and may bully a new horse. When your horse is let out in the field for the first time, there will probably be a lot of galloping about, kicking, and squealing. It could be quite nerve-racking, so watch the commotion for about a half hour to make sure your horse doesn't get hurt. In a couple of days she will establish her place in the pecking order.

Keep a leather halter on for two or three days in case you have problems catching her. Don't use a nylon halter because it will not break if it gets caught on something, and your horse could hurt herself.

Riding Your New Horse

Even if you're eager to ride, give your horse a couple of days to settle in. She needs some time to adjust to her new surroundings and get used to the other horses. At first, she may be excitable and not very well behaved. She may barge in front of you while you are leading her and spook at all sorts of things. When you walk her around the barn, use a chain over her nose so you have extra control. If she is naughty, be firm, but don't lose your temper. You may have to spend a few days working on "ground manners," in other words, leading her around and grooming her.

Spend the first week getting to know your new horse. Visit her every day and groom her. Watch her weight and check her feed bucket daily. Changing barns can upset a horse, and she may not eat as much as usual. If you have changed her feed, she may take a while getting used to it. Start adding a multivitamin supplement to her feed to keep her in good condition. If you bring her a lot of tasty treats such as carrots and apples, she should look forward to seeing you after a few days.

When you finally ride your horse, stay inside an enclosed arena at first. You really don't know how she is going to behave, so it's better to be in a confined space. If you have a riding instructor, have a couple of lessons with your new horse so she can see how you and the horse are getting along. Don't assume that the horse is going to act the same way she did when you rode her at the seller's barn. She may behave completely different in a new environment. It might take a few weeks before you and she become partners. It takes time to get used to each other. As she settles in, her behavior will almost certainly improve. Be patient.

If your horse is really misbehaving, there may be quite a few reasons why. You may need to change her diet. Perhaps she ate a

Grooming is a great way to get to know your horse.

low-energy maintenance feed at her old home and you are feeding her a high-energy, high-protein feed. Maybe she's getting a richer hay than usual.

She might have spent more time outside exercising herself at her old home, while you're keeping her in a stable or pen. You may not be riding her enough. Some horses, especially young ones, need a lot of exercise. Discuss the problem with your instructor and experienced friends, and if it persists, call your veterinarian.

The first time you go on a trail ride, ask a friend who has a calm, experienced horse to come with you. If your horse acts up, you want the other horse to be a good influence on her. Stick to

Ask a friend with a quiet horse to accompany you on your first trail ride.

walking and trotting, or jogging, out on the trail, and see how quickly you can stop your horse before you attempt to canter or gallop in the great outdoors. It's a good idea to alternate walking in front and in back of other horses from the start. Future trail rides will be more pleasant if your horse is happy going first or last.

Have Fun

If you follow most of the advice in this book, you will end up with a decent horse who fits your needs and your pocketbook. You won't make the mistakes many first-time buyers make and buy an unsuitable horse. A good first horse will help you improve your riding skills, and your confidence as a rider will grow in leaps and bounds.

You will be busy as never before. No more sleeping in on weekends—you'll be rushing down to the barn to ride. Mucking out will suddenly become less of a chore because you're doing it for your own horse, and all the inconvenience will be worth the effort—plus you'll develop muscles you never knew you had. You'll be able to go on long trail rides when you want, jump when you please, school at any time, and spend loads of time grooming and pampering your brand-new horse. If you go about it properly, you'll never regret buying a horse.

Here is a sample bill of sale that you might use to purchase your new horse before bringing her home:

BILL OF SALE

This agreement is made between _____,

residing at _____, hereinafter referred to as "BUYER," and _____, residing at

_____, hereinafter referred to as "SELLER," for purchase and sale of the horse described below on the following terms and conditions of sale:

Name: _____ Breed: _____

Age: _____ Sex: _____ Color: _____ Size: _____

A. Consideration

In consideration of the total sum of $_____, SELLER agrees to sell BUYER the horse described above and BUYER agrees to buy said horse on the terms set forth herein.

B. Payment Terms

The BUYER agrees to pay $_____, as deposit on _____ (date), and upon the completion of a satisfactory veterinary examination, will pay the balance of

_____ on _____ , (date) as full purchase price of the horse. Deposit is nonrefundable unless and only if the veterinary examination is not satisfactory with BUYER.

C. Warranties
1. The SELLER warrants that she/he has clear title to the horse.
2. SELLER makes no other warranties, expressed or implied, including the warrantied of fitness for a particular purpose or of merchantability with respect to the health or condition of the horse, its performance abilities or fertility. BUYER accepts the horse as is with all faults.

D. Registration and Ownership Transfers
Upon payment in full, SELLER agrees to execute all necessary papers and to take all steps necessary to transfer ownership and registration of the horse to BUYER at no cost to the BUYER.

E. Risk of Loss
Pending delivery to BUYER, SELLER shall assume the risk of said horse and upon delivery, BUYER shall assume the risk of loss.

F. The Law
The terms of this Agreement and disputes developing thereunder shall be enforced and construed in accordance with the laws of the State of _____. Executed this _____ day of _____, 200_, at _____ time.

Seller

_____ (name)
_____ (address)
_____ (phone)

Buyer

_____ (name)
_____ (address)
_____ (phone)

Resources

American Association of Equine
Practitioners
4075 Iron Works Parkway
Lexington, KY 40511
(859) 233-0147
www.aaep.org

American Connemara Pony
Society
2360 Hunting Ridge Road
Winchester, VA 22603
(540) 662-5953
www.acps.org

American Driving Society
2324 Clark Road
Lapeer, MI 48446
(810) 664-8666
www.americandrivingsociety.org

American Endurance Ride
Conference
P.O. 6027
Auburn, CA 95604
(866) 271-AERC
www.aerc.org

American Farriers Association
4059 Iron Works Parkway
Suite 1
Lexington, KY 40511
(859) 233-7411
www.amfarriers.com

American Hanoverian
Society
4067 Iron Works Parkway

Suite 1
Lexington, KY 40511
(859) 255-4141
www.hanoverian.org

American Holsteiner Horse
Association
222 E. Main Street #1
Georgetown, KY 40324-1712
(502) 863-4239
www.holsteiner.com

American Horse Council
1616 H Street NW
7th Floor
Washington, D.C. 20006
(202) 296-4031
www.horsecouncil.org

American Horse Protection
Association
1000 29th Street
#T-100
Washington, D.C. 20007-3820
(202) 965-0500

USA Equestrian (formerly
American Horse Shows
Association)
4047 Iron Works Parkway
Lexington, KY 40511-8483
(859) 258-2472
www.equestrian.org

American Morgan Horse
Association
P.O. Box 960

Shelburne, VT 05482
802-985-4944
www.morganhorse.com

American Mustang and Burro
Association
P.O. Box 788
Lincoln, CA 95648
(530) 633-9271
www.bardalisa.com

American Paint Horse
Association
P.O. Box 961023
Fort Worth, TX 76161-0023
(817) 834-APHA
www.apha.com

American Quarter Horse
Association
P.O. Box 200
Amarillo, TX 79168
(806) 376-4811
www.aqha.com

American Riding Instructors
Association
28801 Trenton Court
Bonita Springs, FL 34134-3337
(239) 948-3232
www.riding-instructor.com

American Saddlebred Horse
Association
4093 Iron Works Parkway
Lexington, KY 40511
(859) 259-2742
www.asha.net

American Trails
P.O. Box 491797
Redding, CA 96049-1797
(530) 547-2060
www.americantrails.org

American Trakehner Association
1514 West Church Street
Newark, OH 43055
(740) 344-1111
www.americantrakehner.com

American Warmblood
Society
2 Buffalo Run Road
Center Ridge, AR 72027
(501) 893-2777
www.americanwarmblood.org

American Youth Horse
Council
577 N. Boyero Avenue
Pueblo West, CO 81007
(800) TRY-AYHC
www.ayhc.com

Appaloosa Horse Club, Inc.
2720 West Pullman Road
Moscow, ID 83843
(208) 882-5578
www.appaloosa.com

Arabian Horse Registry of
America
10805 East Bethany Drive
Aurora, CO 80014
(303) 696-4500
www.theregistry.org

The Bureau of Livestock
Identification
1220 N Street
Room A-130
Sacramento, CA 95814
(916) 654-0889
www.cdfa.ca.gov/ahfss.li/

CHA - The Association for
Horsemanship Safety and
Education
5318 Old Bullard Road
Tyler, TX 75703
(800) 399-0138
www.cha-ahse.org

Intercollegiate Horse Show
Association
P.O. Box 741
Stonybrook, NY 11790-0741
(303) 450-4774
www.ihsa.com

The Jockey Club
821 Corporate Drive
Lexington, KY 40503-2794
(859) 224-2700
www.jockeyclub.com

National Cutting Horse
Association
260 Bailey Avenue
Fort Worth, TX 76107-1862
(817) 244-6188
www.nchacutting.com

National 4-H Council
7100 Connecticut Avenue
Chevy Chase, MD 20815

(301) 961-2959
www.fourhcouncil.edu

National Hunter and Jumper
Association
P.O. Box 1015
Riverside, CT 06878
(203) 869-1225
www.nhja.com

National Reining Horse
Association
3000 NW 10th Street
Oklahoma City, OK 73107-5302
(405) 946-7400
www.nrha.com

North American Riding for the
Handicapped Association
P.O. Box 33150
Denver, CO 80233
(303) 452-1212
www.narha.org

Palomino Horse Breeders of
America
15253 East Skelly Drive
Tulsa, OK 74116-2637
www.palominohba.com

Performance Horse Registry
4047 Iron Works Parkway
Lexington, KY 40511
(859) 231-6662
www.phr.com

Swedish Warmblood Association
of North America
P.O. Box 788

Socorro, NM 87801
(505) 835-1318
www.wbstallions.com/wb/swana

Tennessee Walking Horse
Breeders' and Exhibitors'
Association
P.O. Box 286
Lewisburg, TN 37091-0286
(931) 359-1574
www.twhbea.com

Trail Riders of Today
P.O. Box 30033
Bethesda, MD 20824-0033
(301) 854-3467
www.trot-md.org

United States Combined Training
Association
525 Old Waterford Road NW
Leesburg, VA 20176
(703) 779-0440
www.eventingusa.com

United States Dressage
Federation
220 Lexington Green Circle
Lexington, KY 40503
(859) 971-2277
www.usdf.org

United State Equestrian
Team
P.O. Box 355
Gladstone, NJ 07934
(908) 234-1251
www.uset.com

United States Pony Club
4041 Iron Works Parkway
Lexington, KY 40511-8462
(859) 254-7669
www.ponyclub.org

United States Team Penning
Association
P.O. Box 4170
Fort Worth, TX 76164-0170
(817) 378-8082
www.ustpa.com

Western Stock Show Association
4655 Humboldt Street
Denver, CO 80216
(303) 297-1166

Glossary

barrel racing: A timed contest in which a mounted rider makes sharp turns around three barrels set in a cloverleaf pattern.

bit: The mouthpiece on a bridle; there are many different types available.

broken: A tamed and trained horse.

bridle: A head harness used to control and guide a horse when driving or riding; usually consists of a headstall and reins with a bit.

canter: A three-beat gait that resembles a slow gallop.

crop: A short riding whip with a looped lash.

cross-pole fence: A fence used for jumping formed by two poles that cross each other, forming an X.

dressage: A form of exhibition riding in which the horse receives nearly invisible cues from the rider and performs a series of difficult steps and gaits with lightness of step and perfect balance. Dressage is also a classical training method that teaches the horse to be responsive, attentive, willing, and relaxed for the purpose of becoming a better equine athlete.

frog: The triangular-shaped horny pad near the rear of the sole of a horse's foot.

gallop: A fast, natural three-beat gait.

halter: A headpiece of leather, rope, or nylon used to lead a horse.

hand: A standard of equine measurement derived from the width of a human hand. Each hand equals 4 inches, with fractions expressed in inches. A horse who is 16.2 hands is 16 hands, 2 inches, or 66 inches tall at the withers.

headstall: The pieces of a bridle including the cheekstrap, throatlatch, browband, and noseband if used.

hock: A joint in the region in the hind leg of a horse that corresponds to a human ankle but bends backward.

hunter: A horse bred and trained to be ridden for the sport of hunting; a show hunter is a horse who is bred to be well mannered and elegant over fences in English classes.

hunt seat: A style of English riding, suited for horses who are hunters and jumpers, based on traditions in the hunt field. In a variety of show classes, hunters are judged on style and manners as they go over jumps, while jumpers are judged on their ability to quickly get over tough obstacles without knocking them down.

lead: The action by the forefoot that takes the first step when entering a canter and while cantering and galloping; a horse on the correct lead is on the right lead when circling clockwise and on the left lead when circling counter-clockwise.

lope: A natural, easy horse gait that is faster than a jog; it has a four-beat rhythm with a pause after the fourth beat.

muck out: To remove manure and soiled bedding from a horse's living area.

neck reining: A way of guiding a horse with reins. A mounted rider holds both reins in one hand (usually the left) and steers the horse by moving the hand in the direction the rider wishes to go, which puts pressure from one rein on the horse's neck.

pedigree: A registry recording a line of ancestors of three generations or more.

purebred: A horse of a distinct breed whose parents are registered in the same studbook without mixture of other breeds.

reining: A western event with origins in ranch work; a reining horse and rider perform a set pattern of movements and gaits, including sliding stops, spins, and rollbacks.

saddle-seat style: A type of riding distinguished by high-stepping gaits.

shipping boots: Thick wraps put on a horse's lower legs to prevent injury during traveling.

show jumping: The competitive riding of horses one at a time over a course of obstacles; horses and riders are judged on ability and speed.

snaffle bit: A type of mild bit.

splints: A condition in which a bony growth forms on the cannon bone (lower leg) of a horse; tearing of a ligament between the cannon bone and a neighboring splint bone causes a hot, painful swelling followed by the formation of a splint.

tack (tackle): Saddle, bridle, and other equipment used in riding and handling a horse.

throatlatch: A bridle strap that goes under the horse's throat.

trot: A natural two-beat gait in which the forefoot and diagonally opposite hind foot strike the ground simultaneously.

turning out: Putting a horse out to pasture.

warmblood: A term used to describe distinct breeds usually named according to the region in which the breed was developed. These large, well-muscled horses possess the calm temperament of their cold-blood draft ancestors and the athleticism of their hotblood forebears, making them suitable for dressage and show jumping.

withers: The highest part of a horse's back, where the neck and the back join.

worm: To rid a horse of intestinal parasites with medication.